The Power of Acceptance

Building Meaningful Relationships in a Judgmental World

by Doug Shadel and Bill Thatcher

Foreword and Epilogue by **M. Scott Peck, M.D.**
Author of the Best-Selling ***The Road Less Traveled***

Viva Books Private Limited
New Delhi • Mumbai • Chennai • Kolkata

First Indian Edition 2003

VIVA BOOKS PRIVATE LIMITED

- 4262/3 Ansari Road, Daryaganj, New Delhi 110 002
  E-mail: viva@vivagroupindia.net

- 215-216 New Apollo Estate, 2nd Floor, Mogra Lane,
  Andheri (E), Mumbai 400 069
  E-mail: vivabooks@mantraonline.com

- 7 Aziz Mulk, Seventh Street, Thousand Lights, Chennai 600 006
  E-mail: vivachennai@mantraonline.com

- 6-A, Rifle Range Road, Kolkata 700 019
  E-mail: vivakolkata@mantraonline.com

Published by arrangement with

Career Press
3 Tice Road
Franklin Lakes
N J 07417
USA

ISBN 81-7649-375-9

Rs. 195

Published by Vinod Vasishtha for Viva Books Private Limited, 4262/3 Ansari Road, Daryaganj, New Delhi 110 002 and printed at Print Perfect, Mayapuri, Delhi.

What People Are Saying About

The Power of Acceptance

By Doug Shadel and Bill Thatcher

"The Power of Acceptance *is a wonderful book, full of healing and hope. It is a guidebook to freedom through authenticity. Using the tools of community building, the authors offer specific steps to breaking the shackles of 'rugged individualism.' An important book for gaining the freedom that is our birthright.*"

—John Gardiner, Ph.D., professor of Educational Leadership, Seattle University

"The Power of Acceptance *is a major ground-breaking contribution to the still-early literature on the subject of community and represents a much-needed new milestone for our exploration of the most vital of frontiers.*"

—M. Scott Peck, M.D., author of *The Road Less Traveled*

"Based on studies of business and neighborhood groups creating community, this warmly crafted book transforms the usual missives about self-help into an uplifting message about reaching out to others. It demonstrates the power of 'hearing each other into speach' and affirms the possibilities of becoming, individually and collectively, our better selves."

—Philip H. Mirvis, professor of Management and author of *The Cynical Americans*

"This outstanding book offers something for both the heart and the head. If you wish to live more authentically, with increasing commitment to personal integrity, and you yearn for meaningful relationships, this is the book for you."

—Mary Ann Schmidt, president of The Foundation for Community Encouragement

Doug Shadel

To my parents, Bill and Julie Shadel,
for always being there when I needed them and
for being the most influential people in my life.

Bill Thatcher

To Jane, my friend, lover and singular companion
for the exciting journey that lies ahead.

Acknowledgments

Doug Shadel

I WOULD LIKE TO EXPRESS MY DEEP APPRECIATION TO THE following individuals without whom this book would not have become a reality: John Gardiner, for his persistent encouragement and guidance in the doctoral program and for introducing me to the workshop model; to ES for her compassionate and insightful nurturing and her rigidly relentless pursuit of what is true and good; to M. Scott Peck, without whose work I would likely be a basketcase and still squirming around at the bottom of the abyss; to my co-author, Bill, for his keen sense of what the everyday individual can hear and learn and for three years of strong support; to Al Saunders and Michele Lanci-Altomare for their professionalism and for making this book the quality product it has become; to Orinda Weiss for her work on the two studies; and finally to Nicholas Shadel for providing me with the inspiration to ask and search for answers to life's most difficult questions.

Bill Thatcher

I WANT TO ACKNOWLEDGE PETE SCHWALM AND JAN WOOD WHO, separately, loved me to such an extent I felt unconditionally accepted. To my daughters, Tauryn and Whitney, I gratefully acknowledge their tolerance and even love as I've struggled to know myself and grow up before their eyes. To my former wife, Anne, who for much of our marriage lived with a spouse unwilling and unable to express his emotions. I wish to acknowledge my co-facilitators at the Foundation for Community Encouragement for their continuing welcome and support of me and especially those I have partnered with in community-building assignments: E.S., Janice, Eve, Scotty, Mary Ann, and Phil. Finally to Doug Shadel, without whose encouragement, prodding and questioning the words you read here would still be inside of me.

Contents

Foreword

MOST RESEARCH IS ABOUT A RELATIVELY ESOTERIC SUBJECT AND virtually unreadable except by specialists highly trained in the subject. But this book is about a subject of potential interest to everyone and, by virtue of its combination of literature and statistical research with anecdotal research, highly readable.

In early December, 1984, my wife, Lily, and I met with nine others to establish the Foundation for Community Encouragement (FCE), a tax-exempt, nonprofit, public, educational foundation. The research findings reported in *The Power of Acceptance* represent far and away the most extensive research to date on this foundation's work over the past dozen years.

It is important to realize from the start that the word *community* as used by our foundation, and reflected in this book, is considerably different from the way it is used by the general public. Generally the word is applied to any geographical aggregate of people, such as Morristown, New Jersey, or else any group with some shared interest, such as a particular church or synagogue. But the reality is that while citizens of Morristown may have a certain tax base and some social services in common, they have precious little else that relates them to each other as individuals.

Similarly, what we find in our churches are people sitting in the same pew together who, with but the rarest of exceptions, are hiding behind masks of composure and unable to talk with each other about their deepest fears, desires, joys and pains.

The concept of community, for us at FCE, is not simply an aggregate of people but a group that has made a commitment to learn how to communicate with each other on an ever more deep and authentic level. In other words, community requires meaningful communication.

And, as an educational foundation (the broader work of the FCE is described in the Epilogue), it is our mission to teach the principles of healthy communication both within and between groups. We teach these principles primarily through a variety of highly experiential workshops called "community-building workshops."

This book centers around the powerful changes in acceptance that people can experience, especially as the result of group participation. Doug Shadel and Bill Thatcher chose to conduct their research for the book by gathering and analyzing data about the experiences of people who have participated in these community-building workshops. Their findings reflect the important and beneficial changes that are almost invariably created when people communicate with intimacy and authenticity.

The beauty of this book is that its authors have not bitten off more than they can chew. Their focus is clear and simple: individual self-acceptance and, by extension, the acceptance of others. I feel the book is a major ground-breaking contribution and represents a much-needed new milestone for our exploration of this most vital of frontiers.

—M. Scott Peck, M.D.

Prologue

THE FOLLOWING STORY HAS BEEN READ AT THE BEGINNING OF most community-building workshops given by The Foundation for Community Encouragement since its inception in 1985. We open this book with it because it provides the core inspiration for the book's contents.

The Rabbi's Gift

There was a monastery that had fallen upon hard times. Once a great order, as a result of waves of anti-monastic persecution in the seventeenth and eighteenth centuries and the rise of secularism in the nineteenth, all its branch houses were lost and it had become decimated to the extent that there were only five monks left in the decaying mother house: the abbot and four others, all over seventy in age. Clearly it was a dying order.

In the deep woods surrounding the monastery there was a little hut that a rabbi from a nearby town occasionally used for a hermitage. Through their many years of prayer and contemplation the old monks had become a bit psychic, so they could always sense when the rabbi was in his hermitage. "The rabbi is in the woods, the rabbi is in the woods again," they would whisper to each other. As he agonized over the imminent death of his order, it occurred to the abbot at one such time to visit the hermitage and ask the rabbi if by some possible chance he could offer any advice that might save the monastery.

The rabbi welcomed the abbot at his hut. But when the abbot explained the purpose of his visit, the rabbi could only commiserate with him. "I know how it is," he exclaimed. "The spirit has gone out of the people. It is the same in my town. Almost no one comes to the synagogue anymore." So the old abbot and the old rabbi wept together. Then they read parts of the Torah and quietly spoke of deep things. The time came when the abbot had to leave. They embraced each other. "It has been a wonderful thing that we should meet after all these years," the abbot said, "but I have still failed in my purpose for coming here. Is there nothing you can tell me, no piece of advice you can give me that would help me save my dying order?"

"No, I am sorry," the rabbi responded. "I have no advice to give. The only thing I can tell you is that the Messiah is one of you."

When the abbot returned to the monastery his fellow monks gathered around him to ask, "Well, what did the rabbi say?"

"He couldn't help," the abbot answered. "We just wept and read the Torah together. The only thing he did say, just as I was leaving—it was something cryptic—was that the Messiah is one of us. I don't know what he meant."

In the days and weeks and months that followed, the old monks pondered this and wondered whether there was any possible significance to the rabbi's words. The Messiah is one of us? Could he possibly have meant one of us monks here at the monastery? If that's the case, which one? Do you suppose he meant the abbot? Yes, if he meant anyone, he probably meant Father Abbot. He has been our leader for more than a generation. On the other hand, he might have meant Brother Thomas. Certainly Brother Thomas is a holy man. Everyone knows that Thomas is a man of light.

Certainly he could not have meant Brother Elred! Elred gets crotchety at times. But come to think of it, even though he is a thorn in people's sides, when you look back on it, Elred is virtually always right. Often very right. Maybe the rabbi did mean Brother Elred. But surely not Brother Philip. Philip is so passive, a real nobody. But then, almost mysteriously, he has a gift for somehow always being there when you need him. He just magically appears by your side. Maybe Philip is the Messiah.

Of course the rabbi didn't mean me. He couldn't possibly have meant me. I'm just an ordinary person. Yet supposing he did? Suppose I am the Messiah? O God, not me. I couldn't be that much for You, could I?

As they contemplated in this manner, the old monks began to treat each other with extraordinary respect on the off chance that one among them might be the Messiah. And on the off, off chance that each monk himself might be the Messiah, they began to treat themselves with extraordinary respect.

Because the forest in which it was situated was beautiful, it so happened that people still occasionally came to visit the monastery to picnic on its tiny lawn, to wander along some of its paths, even now and then to go into the dilapidated chapel to meditate. As they did so, without even being conscious of it, they sensed this aura of extraordinary respect that now began to surround the five old monks and seemed to radiate out from them and permeate the atmosphere of the place. There was something strangely attractive, even compelling, about it. Hardly knowing why, they began to come back to the monastery more frequently to picnic, to play, to pray. They began to bring their friends to show them this special place. And their friends brought their friends.

Then it happened that some of the younger men who came to visit the monastery started to talk more and more with the old monks. After a while one asked if he could join them. Then another. And another. So within a few years the monastery had once again become a thriving order and, thanks to the rabbi's gift, a vibrant center of light and spirituality in the realm.

Introduction

The curious paradox is that when I accept myself just as I am, then I can change.

—Carl Rogers

This book is about developing tools to improve your life in profound ways. While the study of human beings and their interactions with one another is staggeringly complicated, our basic thesis can be boiled down to a fairly simple statement:

> We are born into this world as children of God and are therefore unconditionally accepted. Such acceptance is a fundamental need of human beings. The struggle is that soon after birth, we realize that we live in a judgmental world and that acceptance by others is, in fact, conditional. To gain acceptance, we bury our authentic emotions and feelings and develop "social masks." But ultimately this causes us to become estranged both from ourselves and from one another.

We believe that participation in groups can provide an atmosphere of unconditional acceptance where people can remove their "social masks." Once individuals accept themselves as they are, they can move forward and grow.

We began the research for this book by asking the question, "How does involvement with such groups help people move toward self-acceptance?" We first looked at the literature on individual therapy to find out whether people left the therapeutic relationship feeling better about themselves, and if so, what was it about that relationship that might have made the difference?

Overwhelming, the research showed that the root of the solution was a single "curative factor." That factor was acceptance.

Likewise, the literature on group therapy curative factors also showed that acceptance is a vital arrow in the therapist or group facilitator's quiver. Create a group environment of unconditional acceptance and individuals will thrive and begin to accept themselves and each other. Having identified this major theme regarding what helps people in therapy in general and in group therapy in particular, we were interested to do our own research about how acceptance impacts people in other group settings.

Both of us had become involved in working with a group model called the "Community Building Workshop" sponsored by the Foundation for Community Encouragement (FCE). And while much has been written about this work by FCE co-founder and best-selling author M. Scott Peck, there seemed to be a gap in the literature about the changes people experienced as a result of their participation in this model, particularly over time.

There also seemed to be a gap in terms of hearing first-hand accounts from participants. So we decided to use the example of these workshops to explore just how a group process helps people find acceptance. We conducted two studies of community-building workshop participants. The first surveyed randomly selected individuals who had attended these workshops. We used a 307-question survey designed for part of Doug's doctoral dissertation. Of the 200 people contacted, 31 ultimately completed this extensive survey.

The second study used a 200-question survey given to employees of a very successful, forward-thinking company, Carlisle Motors, a car dealership in Clearwater, Florida. A majority of Carlisle's 600 employees participated in community-building workshops over three years. We contacted 325 of these, and 135 completed the survey. In both studies, the behavioral changes people reported were striking. Key findings are referenced throughout the book, and shown in the appendices.

As with any study, there are limitations to the extent to which conclusions can be broadly applied. In the study of randomly selected workshop participants, the demographics are skewed toward white, upper-middle-class, highly educated Americans, because a high percentage of all attendees of these workshops are from that category. So any conclusions about behavioral change in this study are limited to that population. In the Carlisle Motors' study, the population of respondents was diverse, but not randomly selected. Rather, the company's owners invited people to volunteer for the study. Thus, respondents may have been pre-disposed in one way or another, based upon their interest.

Given these limitations, the two studies seem to complement each other, since the trends are so similar in both and because many of the questions were asked in both studies. What the first study (see Appendix A) lacks in demographic diversity, the Carlisle study provides (see Appendix B). And what the Carlisle study may lack in terms of random selection, the first study provides. The overall result is little variance in the conclusions relating to behavioral change.

While the research results were compelling, we were not satisfied with merely completing an academic study. The cornerstone of effective groups is the individual stories that are shared. It would be hard to find more genuine pouring out of heart and feeling and anxiety and love than that which occurs during one of these workshops. As Ernest Kurtz says in *The Spirituality of Imperfection* (Bantam Books, 1992), the power of storytelling has long been known to have a cathartic effect on the teller:

> Spiritual teachers universally recognized as "great" did not give commandments nor did they impose their way

> of life on others. They knew that when any map was mistaken for the territory, it became more hindrance than help. And so they invited their followers to question the handed-down maps by making available their own maps—their own stories. . . . For they understood what the ancients had discovered: The best way to help me find my story is to tell me your story.

For centuries, the technique of having people tell their stories in a setting of unconditional acceptance has been recognized as a good way for people to shed their masks and begin to feel accepted. So we wanted to convey the real stories of people's experiences. To review the statistics alone without the stories would be, as Scott Peck has said, "like eating an orange that has had all the juice squeezed out of it."

As we thought about how to gather and present people's stories, we struggled with how to convey a phenomenon that is largely experiential. Ultimately, we asked for volunteers who would be willing to tell us about their personal workshop experiences in tape-recorded interviews. Over the past two years we spent hundreds of hours interviewing people from across the United States and Canada. Major portions of these stories are included in this book, giving a human voice to the process of transformation.

It is simply an honor to have listened to these heart-felt, sometimes painful, sometimes awe-inspiring personal accounts. At the same time, we found that people enjoyed the opportunity to tell their stories—to be heard telling their essential truth. In their book *The Feminine Face of God* (New York: Bantam Books, 1991), Sherry Ruth Anderson and Patricia Hopkins describe their interviews with women about spirituality:

> We were "hearing each other into speech," as author and theologian Nellie Morton describes it. For until we can speak our truth and know that we have been heard, we don't wholly know it ourselves. And each time a women told us her story, there was a growing awareness that she, and we, were beginning to find our voices.

It is hard to overemphasize the value of telling one's story as a means of moving toward acceptance. Indeed, one technique sometimes used in current psychotherapy is called "narrative" therapy, which guides the patient through the process of telling and then detaching from old problem stories and re-visioning a new life story that more closely resembles reality.

Between the two surveys and the interviews, we contacted over 700 people as part of our research. The book focuses on individuals whose stories were particularly poignant. Some chose to use pseudonyms so that they could feel more free to speak openly about their experiences.

In this fast-paced world, it is difficult to find our essence. Most spiritual traditions describe the life journey as "leaving home, experiencing the voyage with all of its pitfalls, and returning home." In the journey away from the essential acceptance from which we came, out into the judgmental wilderness of modern culture, the challenge is to find our way back toward wholeness and true acceptance.

We shall not cease from exploration
And the end of all our exploring
Will be to arrive where we started
And know the place for the first time

—*T.S. Eliot* (Four Quartets)

Section One

The Context of Acceptance

Chapter One

Confessions of a Rugged Individualist

Are you there?
Say a prayer for the pretender
who started out so young and strong
only to surrender.

—Jackson Browne

Doug Shadel: When I first heard the story of "The Rabbi's Gift" in 1993 at my first community-building workshop, on Whidbey Island, Washington, I was a card-carrying rugged individualist. I had spent my entire life getting the love and acceptance I needed by being a high-octane performer. I was president of the student body at age 12, top scholar in my class in boarding school in Switzerland at age 13, admitted to and excelled at an exclusive private school in Seattle at 14, was a track star at 17, sailed through four years of college (age 17-21), married a beautiful woman who was my college girlfriend (age 22), got a great job in government running a consumer agency to catch crooked businesses (age 22), earned a master's degree at night (age 24), and had a beautiful son (age 27).

My life was on cruise control and I was winning at everything I did. My parents were financially comfortable, each of high profile in their professions and I was the very embodiment of what was expected from such a family.

I was focused, talented and lucky. I never really thought much about things like feelings and emotions. It wasn't that I wanted to avoid them, it just never came up in my family of rugged individualists. The goal was to kick butt and take names, not talk about weakness and vulnerability. If I encountered someone who was not cutting it, I would judge them, calling them "loser" or "undisciplined" or "idiot." Anyone who wasn't able to make it was a loser. After all, if you couldn't make it in the richest country in the world, the "land of opportunity," you couldn't make it anywhere, and, the logic went, it was your own fault.

To be sure, there was lots of love in my family and not all of my beliefs about rugged individualism came from my parents. Images of the way one should be were and are pervasive in American culture, from the Marlboro Man riding off on his horse into the sunset to Steve Jobs starting Apple Computer in his garage, to Bill Clinton being elected president of the United States at the age of 46. One of my favorite cartoons appeared just after Clinton was elected. It showed two men talking to each other and one said, "The president is 46; you are 48; shouldn't you at least be the CEO of a company or something?"

My images of the way I was supposed to be were in no way made easier by the fact that I had gone to the same high school as Bill Gates, who, like Jobs, had essentially created an empire in the computer business out of nothing; and Gates had gone on to become the richest man in the universe. But then, I figured, he is two years older than me, so there is still time.

The model I grew up with was the same model we all have grown up with: Pull yourself up by your bootstraps, work hard, stay in school and you will move up. For nearly thirty years, this model worked well for me. I had no complaints. I also had no idea of the new world that was about to emerge.

In June, 1985, at the age of 28, my wife and I were expecting our first child. During the middle of her pregnancy, Vicki said to me "You know, Doug, I think you're adopted." I said, "What? You must be having some kind of a hormonal surge or something. What makes you say that?" She went on to explain that she had asked my mother on several occasions what it was like being pregnant and my mother said, "Not bad." She would then ask, "Well, did you get very big?" and my mother would say, "Not really."

In other words, she wasn't really willing to talk about it. Vicki thought this was odd and her intuition told her something was wrong. She told me, "If you ask a woman to talk about her pregnancy, she will usually sit you down and take you through a blow-by-blow account of everything that happened. Your mother doesn't seem to have any interest in talking about it at all." If a woman is not willing to talk about her pregnancy, she reasoned, maybe she never was pregnant in the first place.

Over time, I became curious about this idea. My mother was 45 years old when I was born and she was 43 when my brother was born. But she was always so young-looking for her age, I thought it was possible that she could have had kids at that age. Then I was looking through an old album of photographs one day and I noticed a picture of my mother in a bikini, modeling on the beach in August, 1957, four months before my birth. She looked like a million dollars—and thin. So I asked her about that picture, saying, "If this was in August, 1957, you must have been five-months pregnant at the time." She said, "Yeah, pretty amazing, huh?" I let it go.

Then I was visiting my step-brother one day at his home and I asked him what he knew about the situation. Bill was my dad's oldest son by a previous marriage and a physician in the state department. I asked him if my mother had had any difficulty with her pregnancy. Bill looked a little nervous and then said, "I don't think so, why do you ask?" I said, "Well, I guess the real question is, "Was she ever pregnant?" Bill dodged the question adroitly by saying, "You know, I was out of the country a lot at that time and I didn't see her very much." I noticed that during the rest of that evening, despite the fact that we went on to other subjects, Bill consumed a prodigious amount of cognac.

Bill obviously called my parents and told them that I was asking those sensitive questions. Bill apparently knew how they had been agonizing over their secret. He had known all along of their original decision. Finally, on an evening, ironically, April 1, in 1986, we gathered around the dining room table and they started talking—with hesitation and embarrassment, which was unusual, especially for my dad. But the story had to come out. They started by telling me of what was the second marriage for each of them and of my mother's deep desire to have a child despite her age. She described how one day her obstetrician mentioned a possible adoption. It seems he and a small group of doctors scattered over northern Virginia would take care of unwanted pregnancies within families of acquaintances, offering a temporary home-away-from-home, getting to know the girls and arranging adoptions that would be assuring to both the adopting parents and the girl's family.

As we sat at that dining room table, they described how a surrogate went to the hospital and picked up three-day-old Dave, my brother. Within two years, the same doctor told them of a special birth to come in Winchester, Virginia . . . and that soon thereafter, I came into their home.

In this long, painful evening, they told me how and why they had decided not to tell us of the adoption until we were older . . . perhaps at age eighteen or twenty-one. They said that back in the '50s and '60s, it was debatable whether to tell children about their adoption when the children were young, or wait until they were older. Even their social worker who handled the adoptions favored the latter.

They said they had wanted to tell me earlier, but they could never find a time when they felt it would be accepted by us (my brother was also adopted) without doing significant psychological harm. It became an enormous burden for them. On the one hand, they hated to keep such a secret from their kids, and on the other, they realized that revealing the secret would forever impact us and possibly in a negative way. They also worried that we might reject them for having kept it a secret.

The fact of my adoption was, as Ibsen has called it, "The Vital Lie," a family story that covers up a truth so painful that everyone involved perpetuates it based on their instinct for self-preservation. They simply cannot see how allowing the truth to emerge will help anyone. My parents would later tell me that after about age 21, what had been a strategy they thought would help me really became a secret that they found difficult to confront and, therefore, even more difficult to reveal.

I have since realized that our society is crammed full of "vital lies" and that, in many ways, these lies are at the root of what ails us. We remain intentionally unconscious of truth because we perceive that heightened awareness will mean pain, and no one wants pain.

To say that I was angry when I found out about the adoption would be putting it mildly. My authentic response was to feel betrayed, as though I had been lied to for 28 years and now they had finally come clean and told me the truth. I have since realized that my anger toward my parents was really anger at the realization that I was adopted. They just happened to be available to blame. But at the time, all I could see was rage and anger.

The news of my adoption tore my world apart. As my spiritual advisor ES has said so many times, quoting an ancient proverb, "The truth will set you free, but first it will make you miserable."

The truth made me incredibly miserable. Up until learning about my adoption, I had the world wired. I was on the fast track with literally no obstacles in sight. To be sure, I was a rugged individualist who didn't spend any time thinking about the emotions or feelings I was having, or that anyone else was having for that matter. But it was working for me, so I didn't notice that anything was wrong.

What I did not know or expect was how painful this kind of life can be when the train derails. I went into an emotional and existential tailspin that has lasted the better part of the last ten years. I pursued the search for my birth parents and found my birth mother, my birth father and three wonderful siblings: two half brothers, Hans and Peter, and a half sister, Heidi. But as many adoptees will tell you, finding your family of biological origin is like living through an emotional nuclear explosion. Within nine months of finding them, I was getting divorced.

Contemporaneous with getting divorced, I noticed that there was a dramatic disassociation occurring between me and a number of my fellow "rugged individualist" friends who simply could not cope with this kind of "derailment." I found within a year or so of getting the divorce that I was pretty much completely alone. Among my friends who were still married, most felt awkward inviting me over, so they didn't; my parents, who were deeply traumatized by my hostile reaction to learning about the adoption, moved from Seattle to Phoenix to escape the confrontation of further rejection; my brother was still in town, but he found it difficult to talk about the adoption (as did I); and my birth family lived in New York and was accepting of me, but the relationships were slow to develop and initially filled with emotional tension.

The exception to this pattern of isolation and rejection was my young son, Nicholas, who has been simply a gift from God—there is no other way to put it. I treasure the kind of unconditional love that he has always provided. The fact that Nicholas came along just prior to my learning of the adoption leads me to believe that he was sent to help support me through the rocky waters that lay ahead—he was my first encounter with unconditional acceptance.

And so it was that my path of success using the rugged-individualism model had broken down completely. And I was stunned at how far I fell both in terms of my own self-esteem and in the eyes of my hard-driving, equally successful friends, once they learned of this fundamental failing.

With regard to the latter, I learned very quickly that if you choose rugged individualism, the road of "I can make it on my own without anyone else's help," you are choosing the path of conditional love and conditional acceptance. The fundamental rule of rugged individualism is, "I will accept you as my friend or lover as long as you continue to perform at a level that makes me look good when I am around you." Conditional acceptance. The corollary, but equally important rule of rugged individualism is, "When you fall, there is no safety net. I will drop you like a ton of bricks." I learned the hard way that if you are going to be a rugged individual, you simply cannot fail—or at least you can't admit you failed.

Because the model does not allow failure, one learns to fake it. One learns to develop a persona or social mask that covers up the fact that you are aching inside, screaming for relief from the emotional pain that is lodging right in the center of the heart. I learned that since weakness is unacceptable, I must always show strength, even when I am almost too weak to stand up. The price for not developing such a social mask is the ultimate punishment: judgment and rejection. But there is also a price for wearing the mask all the time and not experiencing feelings: anger, resentment and blaming others.

In any case, I continued to fake it as much as possible. But there were clues that I was changing. Even though I continued to fake it and wear the social mask of strength and perfection, I got vanity license plates that said PRETNDR. I was thinking of the Jackson Browne song: "Say a prayer for the pretender, who started out so young and strong, only to surrender." That was me.

I marveled at the fact that I could have gone 28 years without ever even suspecting a thing about being adopted. In retrospect, I think I didn't get it because I had been taught another essential tenet of rugged individualism: If it's painful, sweep it under the rug. Short of being encouraged along the road of maximum awareness, I was encouraged along the road of minimum awareness. The modeling I received from everyone around me was to hide pain and wear the social mask of having it all together.

But I began to find it more and more difficult to pretend to be strong and stable when clearly I wasn't. The gap between what I was feeling and how I was acting was too great. To use a term used throughout this book, I was living "incongruently."

So my reaction was to isolate myself from others. This was not hard to do, since most of my rugged-individualist friends had already jumped ship, but I further isolated myself even from those who were still willing to interact. I began to see any encounter with another person as a potentially shaming experience. "What if they find out the truth about me, that I was born into this world a bastard child, that my adopted parents were so ashamed of my birth that they kept it from me and the world? And even worse, now that I am damaged goods and don't feel capable of performing at the levels I have been used to, no one will love me. Since I have gotten love in the past by being a superstar, what happens when I am not capable of being a superstar?" I concluded for the longest time that I was just simply doomed.

I isolated myself even from the two people who had shown me the most consistent support of anyone—my parents. For literally years, I could not get over the anger and resentment I felt about the adoption and consequently, I validated their worst fear about telling me of the adoption: that they would be rejected. They did get rejected and, in retrospect, it must have been as painful for them as it was for me.

But it wasn't just my parents. I isolated myself so much that the only contact I had with other people besides my son was with those I absolutely had to deal with to keep my job. I was finding that the abyss of the dark night of the soul seemingly had no bottom and was the scariest place on earth one can ever find.

As we were doing the research for this book, Bill and I discovered some statistics about the surge in isolation and loneliness in America over the past 30 years. For example, the percentage of individuals living alone in America has gone up over 90% since 1960. I wonder how much of this growth in people living alone is the result of individuals isolating themselves as I did from the fear of being judged or shamed by a fairly harsh and critical culture?

After a couple of years of living in the dark night of the soul, I decided that I needed to figure a way out. I had been reading every book I could get my hands on about psychology and adoption and spirituality. I also bought books on tape and tape-recorded lectures, so I could use driving time as efficiently as possible to try to figure this thing out.

My approach to solving problems has always been to use my intellect. I had faith that no matter how messed up my life was, if I could just begin to understand "why" things were the way they were, I could improve them. The most transformational material I found during this time was a series of tape-recorded lectures by M. Scott Peck. I had never read anything by Peck and I certainly had never even heard of *The Road Less Traveled*; after all, I had spent all my time on "the road most traveled" and besides, those kinds of books were off-limits to the rugged-individualism crowd—nothing more than psychobabble, whiny nonsense that was strictly for suckers and wimps (words from the mouth of some of my more hard-core rugged-individualist friends).

Nevertheless, I bought these tapes because I was at the bottom of the abyss. I actually was so far down that I began to say, "I don't care what people think about me, I have to get out of this." In my desperation, I listened to this man who seemed to make sense to me on the most basic gut level. And, most importantly, he seemed to hold no institution or belief structure or philosophy above reproach.

For Peck, there were no sacred cows. He was just doggedly in pursuit of the truth and if that took him across academic disciplines or forced him to question long-held beliefs that one denomination or another considered sacred, so be it. He was a kind of "let the chips fall where they may" author who seemed comfortable with the role of the iconoclastic spiritual tour guide. Little did I know at the time that his books had sold over six million copies and that entire armies of spiritual seekers had been following him for over a decade.

Since all of my heretofore-sacred cows had come back to bite me, I was open to Peck's approach. It turns out that there is a positive side of finding out that you're adopted. One of the gifts is that it can give you permission to wipe the slate clean and begin to freshly evaluate how to live your life.

I derived much healing from Peck's lectures and I eventually read his books: *The Road Less Traveled, A World Waiting to Be Born, The Different Drum, People of the Lie.* And Peck even opened the door for me to start thinking about God. You see, overt dependence on an all-powerful and loving God is also against the rules for the truly rugged individual, which is why I was precluded from even thinking about it. But Peck opened the door to it because he had come from where I had come from: the main-stream. He was a physician and a psychiatrist and clearly a very smart guy, and if it was okay for him to "believe," maybe it was okay for me to.

I can see now what I didn't see then: that Dr. Peck's work would fundamentally change my life; but it would not be his books or lectures that did it. Instead, it would be a silly little weekend workshop, a place where none of my former rugged-individualist friends would be caught dead, I can assure you: doing community building.

I came to my first workshop via John Gardiner, who was the chair of the doctoral program in Educational Leadership at Seattle University at the time. I was accepted into this program in the spring of 1993. I had applied to the program in order to satisfy the yearning I had for a community of learners, people with whom I could share all the lessons and insights I was getting from Peck's work and others.

I decided to defer my enrollment until the summer of 1994, and John told me about a workshop sponsored by the Foundation for Community Encouragement that was taking place in the fall of 1993 on Whidbey Island. He gave me the brochure and I signed up. I really had no idea what to expect from this workshop. I had not yet read *The Different Drum* and

I knew nothing about community building. The only thing I did know was that, at a time when I was in the abyss, Scotty Peck's lectures were like a lifeline for me to hold on to. So I signed up out of faith in this man who seemed willing to extend support to me through his writing even though I had flunked out of the graduate school of rugged individualism.

The day before the workshop, I had had a normal rugged-individualistic kind of day: I had put together a meeting with my former employer, the Washington State Attorney General's office, my current employer, the American Association of Retired Persons, and about seven other government agencies to form a task force on the issue of telemarketing fraud. We met all morning, going around the room discussing what the various agencies could contribute to this joint educational campaign to warn people about fraud.

As usual, most of us had our macho law-enforcement social masks on, with one agency director after another describing all of the great things they had been doing in the past and were committed to doing in the future to solve the problem. I was absolutely no different, chiming in about how now that I ran all consumer programs for AARP in four states and was responsible for some five-million members in those states, I was certain we could nip this problem in the bud. As I remember my impressions of that meeting, I carefully and coldly listened to each person as they spoke and, in my mind, found things to judge about them: what a ridiculous comment that is . . . I can't believe how naive that woman is . . . why does that agency allow such an incompetent person to work there . . . etc.

On the surface however, I was all smiles and "Thank you's," and "See you soon's." The meeting ended with a long list of action steps and program outlines to be discussed at the next meeting.

When I got to Whidbey Island the next day at 9 o'clock, I realized as I was going into the meeting that I didn't know a single one of the forty individuals who were there and, furthermore, I didn't have a clue about what was going to happen. The workshop began as most workshops begin, with all forty participants sitting in a circle of chairs. Two facilitators, Ellen Stephen (ES) and Bill Thatcher, now my co-author, began the meeting by explaining how our time would be spent, and listing some of the rules of community building. They described that we would be in the same room for the next two days in this configuration of chairs and we would be sharing experiences. They indicated that there were not many rules, but there were some guidelines that would help us in our journey toward community.

Bill said that the two biggest barriers to community are speaking when you are not moved to speak and not speaking when you are moved to speak. He also said that the rules included no judging, no fixing, no cross-talk, speak in "I" statements and give your name first whenever you speak.

And with that, ES said, "Now I am going to read a story, and then we will have three minutes of silence. Then if anyone is moved to share something with the group about themselves, they may do so." With this, she read "The Rabbi's Gift," and the workshop had begun. Needless to say, having lived a structured, goal-oriented, activity-filled life up until that point, I was a bit mystified by this whole community-building thing. I am not going to give a blow-by-blow description of what happened in that first workshop, since we discuss the workshop process in detail in Chapters Seven and Eight.

I will say that the experience has transformed my life in profound ways. The over-riding realization for me of that first workshop was: "My God! There is a way to be with other people and not be judged." I even mentioned this observation at some point during the workshop, describing my amazement at how different the first day of the workshop had been from my meeting in the attorney general's office.

I had shared my adoption story with the group during the afternoon of the first day, and at the breaks and during the evening, I was overwhelmed with emotion when person after person came up to me and said, "Thank you for trusting me with your story—it moved me." Thank you for trusting me with your story? Don't you mean, "Thanks for sharing, but now that I know you are a loser, I'm afraid you will have to leave the group." These people were sincerely embracing my truth. The shame-filled secret that had been kept from me for so long and that I had buried behind my social mask for fear of being further shamed was being held up and embraced with love. I realized I had had my second encounter with unconditional acceptance—and it changed me forever.

By the end of the workshop, after listening for three days to other people empty themselves of painful experiences that they had buried deep inside themselves, I began to see the point of the story that begins most community building workshop. The rabbi's "gift" was to help the monks see the divinity inside each one of us and hold it with respect and awe. By the end of the workshop, with most of the social masks and personas stripped away and thrown into a heap in the corner of the room, I began to see the beauty and wonder that lies in each one of us. I began to see that the spirit of the Messiah is really in each of us.

The image that started to come to my mind was the Hindu image of the individual being like a lamp: the light shines brightly in us all, but is more or less visible depending upon the thickness of the lampshade. The lampshade is the persona or social masks I wear to protect myself from the judgmental world. Strip away the judgment and you remove the lampshade (social mask), revealing the brightly shining light within.

The community building workshop showed me the power of forty people sitting together with their lights shining brightly, willing to accept anything that needs to be emptied in order for healing to occur. The intensity of the love and acceptance in the room at the end of this workshop was palpable. It was like returning to the womb, with the warm amniotic fluid gently caressing and protecting you. You needn't do anything in order to be nurtured and supported except breathe in and out and be present and aware.

Individuals who at the start of the weekend had really annoyed me were by the end completely empty of all expectations, judgments and fears and as a consequence, they appeared to me to be almost like saints. I learned that once I strip away the social mask and empty myself of the need to control, judge or fix others, I am free to simply be human—and being a human is a beautiful thing. The ugliness seems to come from engagement with others who have not yet learned the futility and damage caused by the need to control.

And while I myself did not feel like a saint, I sure felt better. I realized that I had been beating myself up and had been far more self-critical than was justified by reality. Not only was I less self-critical, but I felt a lot less judgmental of others. I was flabbergasted at the extent to which the otherwise normal-looking individuals in the room had all experienced tremendous pain and had, like me, been hiding things behind their social masks for fear of being judged. As I later encountered others who had never been to a workshop, I began to realize that everyone has had things happen to them that has caused pain.

The fundamental lesson I learned from that first workshop was the more I judge myself for somehow not measuring up in the world, the more I project that judgment onto others. Conversely, after forty strangers accepted me and my ugly truth about adoption, all of a sudden I began to see others with what one workshop participant called "soft eyes." I began to stop judging my colleagues in the consumer movement who, while clearly posturing during our meeting in the Attorney General's office, were simply doing the best they could. I began to see them with soft eyes because I realized after the workshop that even individuals who look successful have had enormous pain in their lives and to the extent that they act judgmental or harsh or view others with hard eyes, it is because they have beaten themselves up for years.

I began to see my parents with soft eyes, recognizing that they really did love me and that their decision about telling me or not telling me about my adoption was the best they could do at the time. And for those of you out there who may have adopted children and are disturbed by my adoption story, consider this and take hope: At the time of this writing, my adopted parents have become two of my closest friends. Our relationship has gone full-circle—from dependency to autonomy to rejection to friendship and love. We have accepted the adoption and all of its permutations and that has been the key to healing.

The powerful learning then was that individuals each have their own "stuff" to deal with, their own pain, self-judgment and struggles. The trick is not to hide the pain, which is what the school of rugged individualism holds. Rather, the trick is to GET RID OF IT. Unfortunately, many people, like me, are in a Catch 22 because in order to get rid of pain, one must share it with someone else. But to do that is to acknowledge weakness or imperfection (society's definition of imperfection), which preclude many from doing it.

At one point, I asked ES, the FCE facilitator who at the time lived in Seattle, "What if I have some pain that is really bad and

I don't want anyone else to see it?" She said, "When you go to the doctor because you have food poisoning, the doctor's main concern is getting the poison out of you. He doesn't care what it looks like."

I discovered the importance of emptying one's truth because of the forty "instruments of grace" sitting with me during that first weekend in 1993. They were instruments of grace because they modeled for me the unconditional love and acceptance that I believe God provides for me each day. But in this chaotic and noisy world filled with judgment, mixed messages and chaos, we humans need to remind each other of the power of unconditional acceptance. We need to be instruments of grace for each other. And the beautiful thing is, it doesn't seem to matter which side of the transaction you are on; whether you are unconditionally giving or receiving, you are putting yourself in line with truth and distancing yourself from the vital lies that seemed to dominate our world.

The community-building workshops are, for me, like islands of acceptance and truth in an ocean of judgment, and this book is a map of that island. Dr. Peck has given us the guided tour and the model for doing this work, now it is our responsibility to further explore how it works and, in so doing, bring the good news of its healing effects to others in the realm.

This book is our attempt to explore the group process, the continuum between acceptance and judgment and the role community building and group interaction plays along that continuum. Bill and I have been struggling with some of these difficult issues ever since that first workshop where we met, in 1993. We have often discussed how something special happened at that workshop not just for me, but for both of us. We began meeting shortly after the workshop for no particular reason other than to begin to build a friendship and to explore some of the tough issues that this workshop model addresses about human beings and their struggles. This book is the product of those discussions and of many, many interviews with workshop participants and analyses of over 37,000 survey question responses that have been received from individuals all over the United States and Canada who have participated in the community-building workshops.

No description of this first workshop would be complete without further mention of the other facilitator at that first workshop I attended, Ellen Stephen (ES). ES has given her time generously to this project without qualification or remuneration and she has also been willing to give generously even more time to me in the context of spiritual direction and just plain friendship over a three-year period. There is a saying: When the student is ready, the teacher appears. ES came along as a teacher for me at precisely the time when I was ready to learn. She has helped teach me the fundamentals of what it means to be awake, alive and at peace with myself.

Recommended Reading:

Bellah, Robert, et al. 1991. *The Good Society.* New York: Alfred A. Knopf.

Bellah, Robert. 1996. *Habits of the Heart: Individualism and Commitment in American Life.* Berkeley: University of California Press.

Bolen, Jean Shinoda. 1989. *Gods in Everyman: A New Psychology of Men's Lives and Loves.* New York: Harper & Row, Publishers.

Fields, Rick, ed. 1984. *Chop Wood, Carry Water.* Los Angeles: Jeremy P. Tarcher.

Goleman, Daniel. 1985. *Vital Lies, Simple Truths: The Psychology of Self-Deception.* New York: Touchstone Books.

Peck, M. Scott. 1980. *The Road Less Traveled: A New Psychology of Love, Traditional Values and Spiritual Growth.* New York: Simon & Schuster.

Chapter Two

Disconnection and Isolation in America

At first, I viewed our support groups simply as a way to motivate patients to stay on the other aspects of the [heart-disease prevention] program that I considered more important: the diet, exercise, stress management training, stopping smoking, and so on. Over time, I began to realize that the group support itself was one of the most powerful interventions, as it addressed a more fundamental cause of why we feel stressed and, in turn, why we get illnesses like heart disease: the perception of isolation.

—Dean Ornish, M.D.

Is isolation merely perception? As we began to do the research for this book, I wondered whether I was the only "rugged individualist" who had begun to make a transformation away from the climb up the social ladder. I wondered if I was the only person who had gotten divorced and suffered the emotional torture of having to spend a huge part of my life without my son living with me. I wondered if I was the only one who frequently felt desperately lonely and isolated; I wondered if others ever had days so devoid of meaning and motivation that they had trouble getting out of bed to go to work. Was I alone in feeling that everything I had based my previous life on—my persona—seemed now to be an empty lie?

What I found in going to more community-building workshops and reviewing some of the data available on how society has dramatically changed during the last 30 years was that 1) I was not alone and 2) the medical literature is crammed full of evidence of the dangers of such widespread isolation to an individual's health and, conversely, the benefits to social connectedness.

Not only am I not alone, but there is an almost critical mass of individuals in the United States undergoing the pain of personal isolation. It became clear that many people were, like me, yearning for connection with others and not having that need met; unprecedented numbers were isolating themselves by living alone; many people, like me, were getting divorced; and, most disturbingly, there appeared to be a growing number of people who were clinically depressed and even suicidal.

In looking at these data, one caveat is in order. We believe societal transformation is conditioned upon both systemic change and the ability of individuals to transform themselves. I spent the first 17 years of my professional career trying to effect systemic change through working in the state attorney general's office, passing better laws and using the power of government to help people change their behavior. There clearly is a role for this type of activity.

But for my money, it is the latter strategy, individual transformation, that is a necessary pre-condition to social transformation. This is why we have chosen to focus the research in this book on how workshops impact individual behavior as opposed to the effects they may have on systems. Nevertheless, it is important to understand what is objectively known about the changing demographic landscape of America in order to put what we have to say in the proper context.

Carl Rogers once said that human beings are "incurably social" creatures, who yearn for meaningful contact with others. We humans are in the paradoxical situation of needing to develop our individuality while also remaining connected to others. But there is evidence that the pendulum has swung too far in the direction of individualism. Robert Wuthnow, a Princeton researcher, did a national study in 1993 in conjunction with the Gallup organization in which he surveyed some 2,000 individuals and asked them a series of questions about their involvement in small groups. Such groups were broadly defined and included everything from bible-study groups to sewing groups to self-help groups, such as Alcoholics Anonymous.

His findings are reported in a book called *Sharing the Journey* and he has concluded that fully 40% of all Americans belong to some kind of a small group. Perhaps even more significantly, though, Wuthnow and his associates asked this national sample of individuals who belonged to a small group a series of questions about the extent to which they yearn for connection and acceptance by others. For example, he said:

> **I'm going to read you a list of personal needs. For each one, which statement best describes how well you have met that need? Is this a need you have partly met, fully met or never experienced?**

Here are the response percentages:

THE YEARNING FOR COMMUNITY AND ACCEPTANCE

Percentage of group members who have (A) felt each need and (B) met each need fully.

	A	B
Having neighbors with whom you can interact freely and comfortably	93%	43%
Being able to share deepest feelings with someone	94%	57%
Having friends who value the same things in life you do	98%	58%
Being in a group where you can discuss your most basic beliefs and values	98%	66%
Having friends you can always count on when you are in a jam	97%	64%
Having people in your life who are never critical of you	83%	29%
Being part of a group that helps you grow spiritually	90%	53%
Having cooperation rather than competition with people at work	85%	31%
Having people you can turn to when you feel depressed or lonely	96%	62%
Knowing more people in your community	95%	32%

This research is extremely helpful in beginning to quantify the extent to which Rogers's assertion of human beings as incurably social creatures is borne out. While we yearn to be able to get in touch with and accept our true feelings and emotions, as shown by the significant progress individuals make when they are in groups, we also yearn for connection and acceptance from others. It is not surprising that the vast majority of respondents reported that they have experienced the need to "share deepest feelings" or "know more people in the community" or "be in a group where you can discuss your most basic beliefs and values."

What is disturbing is the relatively low percentage of respondents who say they have had that need met fully. The gap between column A and column B is a firm measure of the yearning individuals have for community, connection and acceptance by others. This yearning for connection and acceptance by others is further discussed in Chapter Four and Chapter Five.

There is evidence that the yearning for connection may be greater now than it was a generation ago and may be the result of some very real changes in the social landscape. For example, between 1960 and 1990, the average household has decreased from 3.33 people per house to 2.62 per house, a decline of 21.32 percent. (*Almanac* 1993-1994). Furthermore, the number of one-person households (people living alone) has nearly doubled, growing from 6.8 million (13% of all households) in 1960 to 23.9 million (25% of all households) in 1990, an increase of 92.31 percent.

Another indicator of people living by themselves in increasing numbers is housing. A City of Seattle official said recently that Seattle has a housing crisis not because so many people have moved into the city but because the demand for housing units has skyrocketed due to plummeting average household size.

This move toward more individuals living by themselves is not, in and of itself, indicative of social disconnection. But the combination of a more than 90% increase in those living alone with the high percentage of individuals yearning for more connection according to the Wuthnow survey does appear to indicate that not all of those living alone are happy about it.

Julie is one of those who has lived by herself for most of her adult life and has not been particularly happy about it.

I do yearn to have more people in my life on a more authentic level. If you ask me point blank "have you been lonely," I would say yes. But it comes and goes. And for me, I have found ways of coping with my aloneness. I have never been married, but for a period of time, I was really married to alcohol. I had a relationship with drinking. For the last six years, I have been fat and I think I have had a relationship with food. Now I don't know if it replaced alcohol or not, but first alcohol and now food have been substitutes for human relationships. I was really anesthetizing myself from the pain of my self-imposed isolation.

For example, I will sit down with a bowl of ice cream and the next minute I will look down and the bowl will be empty and I'll say, "Did I just eat that? I don't remember eating that!" I do think I anesthetize myself to numb the loneliness. At least my answer to it has not been a string of the wrong relationships or abusive relationships.

The statistics about obesity that are coming out are frightening and perhaps loneliness is one of the reasons. Food and alcohol very well could be for others, as they have been for me, substitutes for what we all yearn for, which is unconditional acceptance and love.

Participation in an organized group activity can have an impact on an individual's feeling of loneliness. In our survey of individuals participating in community-building workshops, fully 65% said that prior to the workshop, one of the things that bothered them was feeling lonely. This figure dropped to 57% after participating in the workshop and later, to 30%.

One of the phenomenon that is clearly driving this move toward more social isolation is divorce. Between 1972 and 1990, the percentage of people in the United States who are divorced grew from 3.2 percent of the population to 8.8 percent of the population, a 175% increase. This increase has been studied by many sociologists. It has also been used as a football by both political parties, which accuse each other of causing the break-up of the family based upon systemic changes the other has initiated. Regardless of why this phenomenon has occurred, it has clearly altered the landscape of American life during the past generation.

Many people in workshops bring up divorce as a key trigger for them in their spiritual journey or personal transformation and there are a number of stories from such individuals in the pages that follow. This topic also is addressed in Chapter Four.

Another statistic that suggests there has been an increase in social isolation among individuals is that between 1970 and 1992, the percentage of the population that has never been married grew from 18.9 percent to 26.2 percent of the population, a 38% increase.

Robert Putnam, a Harvard University political scientist, wrote an article in 1995 entitled, "Bowling Alone: America's Declining Social Capital," in which he reviewed additional data that implied that society is becoming more and more disconnected. The inspiration for his title was based on the fact that while the number of individuals who bowl in the United States increased from 51.8 million in 1970 to 82 million in 1992, the number of people who belong to bowling leagues has dropped from 7.73 million in 1970 to 5.88 million in 1992, a decrease of 24%.

This decline is of economic importance to those who own bowling alleys, says Putnam, because the profit from bowling alleys is in the beer and pretzels that bowlers buy on bowling league night. Individual bowlers consume far less beer and pretzels, apparently. Putnam also points out that in almost every area of community engagement, the United States has experienced declining levels of participation.

Here is a sample of the statistical evidence to which Putnam refers. The primary sources for this and the above data are the *General Social Survey (GSS)* and *The American Almanac: Statistical Abstract of the United States.*

- ▲ One measure of social connectedness is the extent to which people spend a social evening with neighbors. Between 1972 and 1994, the number of people saying they spent a social evening with a neighbor at least once per week dropped from 22.1% of all respondents to 16%, a decline of 16% *(GSS).*
- ▲ The percentage of people belonging to fraternal organizations like Elks clubs and Lions clubs has declined 35% between 1974 and 1988, from 14% to 9% of the population (Caplow, et al., *Recent Social Trends*).
- ▲ In 1973, 22 percent of Americans attended a public meeting on town or school affairs. In 1993, it was 13%, a decline of 41%.
- ▲ Parent-Teacher Association (PTA) membership had an aggregate membership of 12 million in 1964. In 1994, the number was 7 million, a decline of 42% *(GSS).*
- ▲ Overall church membership as a percentage of the population has gone from 63.3% in 1960 to 59.3% in 1990, a decline of 6%.

As a political scientist, Putnam's interest in the subject of individuals not connecting is focused less on the implications of such demographic change on the individual and more on the communities in which the individuals live and work. The loss of civic engagement or, as Putnam calls it, "social capital" in any one community can have a negative effect on the health of the community.

Putnam saw this in Italy when he and a number of his colleagues at Harvard began a longitudinal study some thirty years ago of four communities in Italy, each of which had installed the same type of government structure. The research opportunity, as Putnam and his associates saw it, was to study how the same political system would work when it was applied to four completely different communities. The results of this study are contained in a book by Putnam entitled *Making Democracy Work.*

One of the assumptions made going into this study was that some of the communities that were the most successful had developed civic organizations, such as choral societies and Rotary Clubs. They assumed that those civic organizations thrived because the economy of the community was thriving. What they found after careful analysis of these four communities in Italy over three decades was that their assumptions were precisely backwards. Economic vitality was not a pre-condition of civic engagement; civic engagement was a pre-condition of economic vitality. Therefore, when civic involvement declines, one worries that economic decline might not be far behind.

For our purposes, such decline in civic engagement, together with more and more people living alone and the apparent yearning for community and connection, raises even more questions about what is going on in this country inside the psyche of the individual. Concern for the impacts on government and systems is important, but one cannot ignore the impact on any one individual of such isolation.

One thing that we do know is going on contemporaneous with such civic disengagement is a decline in trust, both of others and of institutions. According to the *GSS,* which is an annual survey given to the same individuals each year by the Roper National Public Opinion Research Center, there has been a dramatic decline in the extent to which people in the United States trust one another. Roper asked, "Can most people be trusted?" In 1960, 58% of those surveyed said yes. In 1993, 37% said yes. This represents a decline of 36% over the past thirty years.

The correlation between social isolation and reduced trust is troubling but will make more sense as we discuss the conditional love culture, the implications of women in the work force and the logic of the marketplace pervading every aspect of our existence.

When asked by the Roper organization, "Have you 'Never or almost never' trusted the government?" in 1966, 30 percent said yes and in 1992, 75 percent said yes. This represents an increase of 140% in the number of people who distrust government.

Another particularly disturbing statistical trend is the suicide rate in the United States. The suicide rates for white males has grown from 18 per 100,000 population in 1970 to 22 per 100,000 population in 1992, an increase of 22%. The increases were most acute among 15- to19-year-old white males and those over 85 years old.

For Americans born before 1905, the rate of those having a major depression over a lifetime was just 1 percent. For those born since 1955, by age twenty-four about 6 percent had become depressed. For those born between 1945 and 1954, the chances of having had a major depression before age thirty-four are ten times greater than for those born between 1905 and 1914 (Goleman, *Emotional Intelligence*).

Another indicator of increases in mental disorders is that in 1955 there were 1.7 million instances of clinical intervention involving mental patients in the United States; by 1975, there were 6.4 million (Csikszentmihalyi, *Flow*).

So what?

One must at some point stop and say, "So what?" Why is it important to know about all these statistics that show more and more people choosing to live alone even though they yearn for connection? Who cares? If more people want to live alone, let them—it's a free country. Notwithstanding the public interest reasons for concern about this that Putnam and others have articulated, as we began this chapter suggesting, the extent to which individuals feel connected to others is enormously important to their emotional and physical health.

Vast amounts of research have been conducted by the National Institute of Health and others that clearly demonstrate the health benefits of social connectedness.

To cite just one such study, a University of Michigan research team found that "people with the weakest social ties have significantly higher death rates—100 percent to 300 percent for men, 50 percent to 150 percent for women—than their counterparts who are more socially integrated in terms of marital and family status, contacts with friends, church memberships and other group affiliations." *(Creating Community Anywhere).*

Dr. Dean Ornish, author of *Dr. Ornish's Program for Reversing Heart Disease,* having conducted major research on heart disease patients and the role of support groups, is absolutely convinced of the importance of social connectedness in maintaining good health:

> In short, anything that promotes a sense of isolation leads to chronic stress and often, to illnesses like heart disease. Conversely, anything that leads to real intimacy and feelings of connection can be healing in the real sense of the word: to bring together, to make whole. The ability to be

intimate has long been seen as a key to emotional health; I believe it is essential to the health of our hearts as well.

Research conducted by a team from the University of Texas School of Public Health in 1996 supports Ornish's belief in the importance of social support and community to good health. The team collected data on 292 Mexican-Americans and 304 non-Hispanic whites who had survived a heart attack longer than four weeks. They found that the patients who had no spouse or close friend to encourage them were 89% more likely to die within three-and-a-half years after a heart attack than patients who had such support. (*USA Today,* Jan. 30, 1997, quoting the *Journal of Behavioral Science*).

The research on the health benefits of social connectedness verify a phenomenon that I observed in the mid-1980s with so-called life-care facilities for senior citizens. These facilities were created to give seniors peace of mind as they approached the end of their lives by offering a full-service retirement home that would provide various services to them as they age: everything from minimal housekeeping to acute nursing home care. In exchange for this promise, the facilities charged a one-time fee, usually in the hundreds of thousands of dollars, plus monthly rent. The up-front fees were calculated based on the life expectancy of the client.

Unfortunately, a number of these facilities went bankrupt during the first ten years of their existence. While working as an investigator in the attorney general's office, I interviewed the owners of these firms and reviewed their books to see why they went under. The consistent answer was this: A majority of the residents outlived all the actuarial predictions for life expectancy because they were so happy and healthy living in a community with others their own age! So one moral of this story is that if you want to maximize the length and quality of your life, figure out a way to stay connected with other human beings.

Additional studies have been conducted on the health benefits of volunteering. These studies show that individuals who spend time volunteering for the good of others may significantly extend their life expectancy. Unfortunately, as we will discuss in more detail in Chapter Four, we have become a fairly egocentric and instant-gratification society that focuses almost all of its attention on materialistic gain. In addition, because the typical American is so busy struggling to make ends meet, we are experiencing what Michael Lerner has called "shrinking circles of concern." We are so busy taking care of ourselves and our immediate family that we can't afford to help others. This reduces the opportunity not only to help one another, but even to interact with one another, causing further isolation and disconnection.

Simply put, it appears that our culture, for whatever reasons, is promoting "a sense of isolation," as Dr. Ornish describes it, which can and does lead to illness. Unprecedented numbers of Americans are choosing to live by themselves and are isolated from others who could provide support and acceptance and healing.

If you read this chapter and can relate in your own life to the statistics we have reviewed, then read on. How we escape from the traps of our culture is the subject of the rest of this book.

Recommended Reading:

Bennett, William. 1994. *The Index of Leading Cultural Indicators.* New York: Touchstone Books.

Ornish, Dean. 1990. *Dr. Ornish's Program for Reversing Heart Disease.* New York: Random House.

Putnam, Robert. 1995. "Bowling Alone: America's Declining Social Capital." *Journal of Democracy.*

Putnam, Robert. 1993. *Making Democracy Work: Civic Traditions in Modern Italy.* Princeton: Princeton University Press.

Shaffer, Carolyn R. and Anundsen, Kristin. 1993. *Creating Community Anywhere: Finding Support and Connection in a Fragmented World.* New York: Putnam Publishing Group.

Wuthnow, Robert. 1994. *Sharing the Journey: Support Groups and America's Quest for Community.* New York: The Free Press.

Chapter Three

The Search for the Authentic Self

Our deepest fear is not that we are inadequate.
Our deepest fear is that we are powerful beyond measure.
It is our light, not our darkness, that most frightens us.
We ask ourselves, who am I to be brilliant,
gorgeous, talented and fabulous?
Actually, who are you not to be?
You are a child of God.
Your playing small doesn't serve the world.
There's nothing enlightening about shrinking so that
other people won't feel insecure around you.
We were born to make manifest the glory of God
that is within us. It's not just in some of us;
it's in everyone. And as we let our own light shine,
we unconsciously give other people permission
to do the same. As we are liberated from our own fear,
our presence automatically liberates others.

—Nelson Mandela, 1994 Inaugural Speech
(from Williamson, A Return to Love)

WHEN NELSON MANDELA MADE HIS INAUGURAL SPEECH IN 1994, he was addressing a nation that had been subjected to apartheid for nearly fifty years. In this country, apartheid meant that out of 45 million people, 5 million white and 40 million black, 90% of the total population was institutionally discriminated against and made to feel as though they were less than second-class citizens.

Mandela himself was in prison for 27 years as a political prisoner, during which time he contemplated the nature of man and his dilemma. The statement above expresses the essence of what Mandela considers to be people's potential and the barriers to achieving that potential: the fear of our own power. The fear of "letting our light shine" can be tied to the wounds many of us have received when we did "let our light shine" and were rejected by others.

This chapter addresses the dualistic nature of our reality and the struggle to connect the dark and the light; the vertical realm (human being in relation to the divine ground of being) versus the horizontal realm (human being in relation to human being); and the essential self with the existential social self. We will also look at the contribution psychotherapy has made to overcoming these dualisms via the intentional surfacing of previously hidden emotions and feelings. These topics provide additional context and theoretical underpinnings for the description of community building and the research that is reported upon later in this book.

The Theology of Acceptance

As the authors of this book, our personal theology includes certain essential core beliefs. We understand that each person reading this book carries their own belief system. The purpose of this book is not to change your beliefs. Rather, it is our wish that you will find within your belief system principles of acceptance, commitment and love similar to those we describe in the following section.

It may be that we fear our own power as Nelson Mandela has said, but another possibility is that we have simply lost sight of or become estranged from that power. Paul Tillich, one of the most prominent Christian theologians of the twentieth century, makes this point in his classic three-volume work entitled *Systematic Theology.*

Tillich's primary thesis and contribution to twentieth-century thought is the idea that God is not a being separate from other beings, but that God is being itself. To the extent, therefore, that we are essentially beings, we come from and have within us divine essence. And that divine essence is good. As Augustine affirmed, "esse quo esse bonum est," which means, "Being as being is good." (*Carl Rogers: Dialogues*). According to the biblical word, "God looked at everything he had created and behold! it was very good."

The dilemma is that we become estranged from this essence. Part of the imprint of the Creator on creation is the echo of this unconditional acceptance as found in the pronouncement of creation being "very good." There is a yearning in the heart for what once was, but is no longer, reachable within. Unable to repair this divine estrangement, we seek instead to soothe that divine ache through others. But with each one of us seeking to fill the same spot, it is difficult, if not impossible, to give what you perceive you do not have.

M. Scott Peck, in *A World Waiting to Be Born,* described God's love for us as a covenant and pointed out that a covenant is not the same as a contract, which is, by definition, conditional. A covenant is an unconditional commitment and God has given all individuals such a commitment, the significance of which is hard to overstate:

> It is hard to trust unconditional love. But we have the power of choice. Just because it is there doesn't mean we have to accept a covenant or believe in it. We can turn away from it. But since it is there, unconditionally, we always have the right to change our minds and return to it. These points are critical, for it is within the context of God's covenantal relationship with us that the call to civility exists. We can accept or we can reject our true vocations. We can choose to hear and attend to the still small voice of conscience or God. It is also within our power to refuse to hear and ignore it.

Throughout history, we humans have simply forgotten this unconditional commitment of love or have become estranged from it. As Peck suggests, it is extremely difficult to remember that we are unconditionally loved and accepted by our Creator when all around us in the existential world we find conditionality and judgment.

This divine purpose, to love oneself and one's neighbor and one's enemy, becomes possible out of re-creation that has taken place with the removal of one's estrangement from God. Yet it is often forgotten or denied and in its absence we spend inordinate amounts of time seeking to do things to get that which we both need but already possess: acceptance.

If the fundamental struggle of men and women on this earth is coping with their estrangement from their divine origin, then acceptance is the doorway to reconnecting or reuniting with both the essential nature of themselves and of others.

The Psychology of Acceptance

Psychology can teach us much about our authentic self and the extent to which our estrangement has blinded us from the truth of our blessed essential reality. It can also provide us with a road map for locating it.

In an enlightening series of dialogues in 1965 in Chicago, Paul Tillich and Carl Rogers addressed the issue of man's estrangement from his essential self and the relationship of psychotherapy to the amelioration of such estrangement. Rogers, whose person-centered therapy made him one of the best known psychologists in modern times, has a theory that parallels Tillich's construction of the essential/existential estrangement.

Rogers believed that human beings as organisms are in a perpetual state of "becoming" and that the natural direction of that becoming is toward wholeness. However, this process of becoming is frequently disturbed or blocked by the external environment that forces individuals to deviate from the natural state of moving toward wholeness, in order to get the short-term love and acceptance that is so vital to us. Rogers, like Tillich, says the individual becomes "estranged" from his authentic self. In *Dialogues,* he says:

> The infant is not estranged from himself. To me, it seems that the infant is a whole and integrated organism, and the estrangement that occurs is one that he learns—that in order to preserve the love of others, parents usually, he takes into himself as something he has experienced for himself, the judgments of his parents: just like the small boy who has been rebuked for pulling his sister's hair goes around saying "bad boy, bad boy." Meanwhile, he is pulling her hair again. In other words, he has introjected the notion that he is bad, where actually he is enjoying the experience, and it is this estrangement between what he is experiencing and the concepts he links up with what he is experiencing that seems to me to constitute the basic estrangement.

In other words, the individual, in the quest for love and acceptance, deserts his own experience to take on a way of being that will bring love. This results in a feeling of being cut off from one's own deeper meaning. But in the 1990s, the way of being that will bring love changes frequently and thus the individual struggles to know how to be, in order to gain acceptance, and can at times feel like a cork bobbing in an ocean of judgment.

Numerous studies have been conducted with people prior to, during and after they have participated in psychotherapy. In most instances, the conclusion is that the gap between how the patient perceives himself and how he would describe his ideal self narrows. When I first read these research findings, which were conducted in Chicago by Carl Rogers and his associates and the Chicago Institute for Mental Health, I thought, "Okay, that makes sense. People begin to get more realistic about who they should be and so they lower their definition of the ideal self, thereby closing the gap between the perceived and the ideal self." But I was wrong!

The research consistently shows that patients in therapy do, in fact, close the gap between the perceived and the ideal self, but it is not the result of the ideal self being lowered; it is the result of their self-perception being raised! This research shows that therapy can have the effect of helping individuals see that they are really much closer to the self they want to be, their ideal self, than they realized.

Part of the explanation for this takes us back to the ocean of judgment in which most of us live. In the Rogerian school of psychotherapy (and in most others as well), the principle goal is not to lecture the patient about why he or she should come to see his or her own self worth. The goal is simply to create an environment of unconditional acceptance, in which the patient can begin to look with clear eyes at what is going on for them.

By creating a safe, judgment-free environment, the therapist helps the patient remove a lot of the negative self-talk and the layers upon layers of psychological defenses that people develop to protect themselves from the harsh realities of our judgmental culture. In so doing, the patient is able to embrace some of the deeply buried emotions and feelings that have been previously unacceptable, and incorporate them into awareness.

The Psychology of Groups

Given the positive impact of individual psychotherapy in helping people to find self-acceptance and in connecting with others, we wanted to review the impact of group therapy on these same issues. How does participation in groups improve people's ability to find acceptance in the culture of conditional love and judgment? To answer this question, we reviewed the conclusions of some of the world's prominent psychologists and researchers on the subject. The simple overview that follows is provided to give a context for the community-building workshops that are used in this book to show the way groups work.

Various kinds of encounter groups have emerged ever since the first so-called T-group ("T" for training) was held in 1946 in Connecticut. These groups were sponsored by the State of Connecticut, which had just passed a Fair Employment Practices Act and was looking at new ways in which work environments might be improved. Later, in 1950, the National Training Laboratory was created as the primary sponsoring agency of T-groups as a department within the National Education Association.

Since those first T-groups, the different types of "self-help" groups that evolved ranged from small discussion groups to large encounter groups:

- T-Group—emphasizes human relations skills
- Encounter Groups—emphasizes personal growth
- Sensitivity Training Groups—can resemble either of above
- Task-Oriented Groups—focuses on tasks usually in an industrial setting
- Sensory Awareness Groups—emphasizes physical awareness
- Creativity Workshops—creative expression through art
- Organizational Development Groups—focuses on skills in leading people
- Team Building Groups—used in industry to develop teams
- Gestalt Groups—focuses on an expert in gestalt therapy treating one person at a time in a group
- Synanon Groups—focuses on drug treatment using shock attacks on the defenses of a person.

Rogers observes that the main goal of such groups is "the facilitation of the expression of both feelings and thoughts on the part of group members. . . a psychological climate of safety in which freedom of expression and reduction of defensiveness gradually occur."

The literature on groups seems to indicate that the goal of group participation is frequently to foster a lowering of the psychological defenses in order to reveal previously abandoned or repressed aspects of the self. Being in a warm, non-threatening, non-judgmental environment allows group members to feel free to look deeply within themselves and to bring forth previously forbidden thoughts or feelings that they had deemed to be unacceptable, and share them with the group in order to begin to integrate and accept them as part of who they really are.

Irving Yalom, in his classic work *The Theory and Practice of Group Psychotherapy,* outlines the principle sixty "curative factors" that people have reported are most helpful to them in group therapy settings. Here are the top ten of these sixty factors. With the exception of the first one (self-acceptance), all these factors relate in some way to the individual's ability to be accepted by or be accepting of other people.

THE TOP-TEN ON YALOM'S CURATIVE FACTORS LIST

1. Discovering and accepting previously unknown or unacceptable parts of myself.
2. Being able to say what was bothering me instead of holding it in.
3. Other members honestly telling me what they think of me.
4. Learning how to express my feelings.
5. The group's teaching me about the type of impression I make on others.
6. Expressing negative and/or positive feelings toward another member.
7. Learning that I must take ultimate responsibility for the way I live my life no matter how much guidance and support I get from others.
8. Learning how I come across to others.
9. Seeing that others could reveal embarrassing things and take other risks and benefit from it helped me to do the same.
10. Feeling more trustful of groups and of other people.

Rogers and Yalom suggest that the environment created in a group setting shares the main characteristics of that created in individual therapy. Rogers says the three characteristics of an effective therapist are that he or she be congruent (authentic in terms of feelings and actions), provide unconditional positive regard for the patient and be empathetic. In a group setting, it is the group that must create the same kind of atmosphere as a therapist does in individual therapy. Yalom suggests that a critical prerequisite for such support to occur is a quality he calls "group cohesiveness."

Perhaps one of the best early reviews of the literature on encounter groups was done by researcher Jack R. Gibb. He reviewed studies done on nine different types of encounter groups. Gibb reports that some of these studies addressed the question: "Do encounter groups facilitate greater self-understanding and acceptance? His review showed that groups had "a greater tolerance for new information and greater acceptance of difference."

Gibb also reports that an increase in congruence between the ideal self and the actual self reflects a positive change in the individual's view of his or her actual self—not a change in the ideal self. To that extent, improvements in congruence can be interpreted as a change in self-esteem or self-acceptance.

The question of what is it in a group that causes self-acceptance to improve was addressed by Mark King and David Payne. They point out that *most individuals perceive more negative self-traits than do outside observers.* As group members begin to explore themselves in a nurturing and accepting environment, many realize they are not the only ones who have inadequacies, and that many of the things they had hidden from others for fear of being ashamed were in fact commonly held "secrets." This makes the task of accepting oneself and integrating such previously forbidden things into the conscious self easier.

A study by Rugal (1990) looked at the relationship between acceptance of self and denial in a DUI recovery group. He reviewed the extent to which group therapy helped early-stage alcoholics integrate previously rejected alcoholic aspects of themselves. Rugal used Yalom's Curative Scale but sought to measure relationships between each curative factor and changes in denial on the part of alcoholics as a result of participation in a 12-week counseling group. He found a positive correlation between group acceptance and self-acceptance, indicating that those who experienced the greatest group acceptance also experienced the greatest self-acceptance.

A recent study on encounter groups that relates directly to community building is an unpublished master's thesis done by Lysle Evans Betts in 1995, entitled, "The Impact of M. Scott Peck's Community Building Workshops on Levels of Self-Esteem and Moral Reasoning of Participants."

Betts, in cooperation with the FCE, studied three community-building workshops. Betts was interested in determining what role, if any, this workshop might have in changing self-esteem. She found that the average scores improved by a 2.57-point gain on the Tennessee Self-Concept Scale, which represents a jump in the average score from the 60th percentile to the 80th percentile. Betts cautions that there is a danger of making a causal link between the two scores without conducting more research and without having a control group. She also points out that further study must occur to determine whether these marked improvements in self-esteem last over time. But she does conclude that ". . . these findings strengthen the idea that successful community building experiences may facilitate positive personality change."

These studies of group therapy reveal some pretty significant benefits that participation in group therapy and/or encounter groups may have for individuals. Participation in groups seems to help people move in the direction of acceptance and away from the self-blame and judgment which gets so many of us in trouble.

A central theme of this book is that much of the conflict we have with each other and even within ourselves relates to the layers and layers of existential defenses, masks and personas that we use to protect ourselves from judgment. Once such armor is removed, both patients and therapists often find that they very much like what lies underneath: the authentic self.

Another important theme here is the idea that self-acceptance is dependent on acceptance by others. Rogers says, "I believe the person can only accept the unacceptable in himself when he is in a close relationship in which he experiences acceptance. This is a large share of what constitutes psychotherapy—that the individual finds that the feelings he has been ashamed of or that he has been unable to admit into his awareness, that those can be accepted by another person, so then he becomes able to accept them as part of himself." *(Dialogues).*

Paul Tillich makes the same assessment: "The man-to-man experience of acceptance of the unacceptable is a very necessary pre-condition for self-affirmation." Only by accepting oneself fully can we begin to move toward wholeness and healing and begin to approach the potential for greatness that Nelson Mandela so eloquently spoke of during his inaugural address in 1994.

Conclusion

Humanity's struggle, then, is to break through the wounds and fears of the existential world and risk looking deeply inward to locate and embrace the authentic self that is in us all. This takes great courage because it means adventuring into the unknown. But stepping into the abyss of the unknown, as I have discovered through my own journey, is the only way to rid oneself of the armor that is a barrier to the divine.

As long as the shields of defense are up, the keys to the kingdom remain hidden. Let down your shields and the key to the world will present itself before you. That key is acceptance and love.

Recommended Reading:

Buber, Martin. 1958. *I and Thou.* New York: Macmillan Publishing.

Campbell, Joseph, in conversation with Bill Moyers. 1988. *The Power of Myth.* New York: Anchor Books/Doubleday.

Campbell, Joseph, in conversation with Michael Toms. 1989. *An Open Life.* New York: Harper & Row, Publishers.

Kierkegaard, Soren. 1962. *Works of Love.* New York: Harper Touch Books

Kirschenbaum, Howard, ed. 1989. *Carl Rogers: Dialogues.* Boston: Houghton-Mifflin Company.

May, Rollo, ed. 1958. *Existence: A New Dimension in Psychiatry and Psychology.* New York: Basic Books.

May, Rollo, ed. 1961. *Existential Psychology.* New York: Random House.

Peck, M. Scott. 1993. *A World Waiting to Be Born: Civility Rediscovered.* New York: Bantam Books.

Rogers, Carl R. 1951. *Client-Centered Therapy.* Boston: Houghton-Mifflin Company.

Rogers, Carl R. 1961. *On Becoming a Person: A Therapist's View of Psychotherapy.* Boston: Houghton-Mifflin Company.

Tillich, Paul. 1957. *Systematic Theology, Volume II.* Chicago: University of Chicago Press.

Tillich, Paul.1952. *The Courage to Be.* New Haven: Yale University Press.

Yalom, Irving D. 1975. *The Theory and Practice of Group Psychotherapy.* New York: Basic Books.

SECTION TWO

Barriers to Acceptance

Chapter Four

The Culture of Conditional Love

The '80s were about acquiring—
acquiring wealth, power, prestige. I know.
I acquired more wealth, power and prestige than most.
But you can acquire all you want and still feel empty.
What power wouldn't I pay for a little more time
with my family! What price wouldn't I pay
for an evening with friends!
It took a deadly illness to put me eye to eye
with that truth, but it is a truth that the country,
caught up in its ruthless ambitions and moral decay,
can learn on my dime. I don't know who will lead us
through the '90s, but they must be made to speak
to this spiritual vacuum at the heart of
American society, this tumor of the soul.

—Lee Atwater
("Lee Atwater's Last Campaign," Life, *February 1991)*

AT THE TIME LEE ATWATER MADE THIS STATEMENT, HE HAD brain cancer and only months to live. But throughout the 1980s he was considered to be an incredibly successful person, advising presidents, winning elections and as chairman of the Republican National Committee, effectively wielding more political power than just about anyone else. The disillusion that he articulates above was brought on by the imminence of his death, but is an emotion that nevertheless lingers inside many of us.

It represents the essential estrangement that Paul Tillich speaks of in the previous chapter and it has never been more prevalent than it is in the 1990s. The utter preoccupation we have with success, money and materialism and the alluring and mind-numbing effects of powerful technology has created a cultural noise that threatens to drown out anything even remotely resembling unconditional acceptance.

Simply put, we live in a conditional-love world: a world where my willingness to be civil to you is conditioned on what you can do for me. There are five primary manifestations of this conditional existence:

1. People as instruments of commerce
2. The idolatry of materialism
3. Zero-sum competition
4. Image perfection
5. The outer-directed person.

1. People as Instruments of Commerce

I described in Chapter One the sense I had when I was meeting with other government officials the day before my first community-building workshop. My overwhelming impression was that each of us was behaving insincerely. We were engaging in one of the oldest practices in human existence: You scratch my back and I'll scratch yours. As I thought about my own life, almost everyone I knew was someone I could get something from. As I became aware of this phenomenon, it appeared to be everywhere.

As a consumer advocate, I regularly participate in meetings between the private sector and government regulators to discuss problem areas. The world views of these two groups couldn't be farther apart. Those who make their living selling things to consumers have become enormously sophisticated at researching everything there is to know about their customers: likes, dislikes, spending habits, lifestyle habits, sleeping patterns, eating patterns.

To the legitimate business person, such research is done to better serve the customer. To the illegitimate business person, it is information that is used to exploit the consumer. Either way, there is an extent to which the consumer is dehumanized, objectified, viewed really as nothing more than an instrument of commerce.

This way of viewing humans as instruments of commerce is also observable at another kind of institution: the business club. For four years, I traveled the state of Washington attending Rotary Club meetings and other business-types of gatherings. These meetings and organizations have very fine humans beings in them. In fact, many of the best people in business are the ones who belong to service clubs and they do an awful lot for their communities. Yet, here you can observe the objectification of humans as instruments of commerce, because what is referred to as a "networking session" is really an overt manifestation of humans as business units.

It is not the individual business man or woman who is to blame for the objectification of humans as instruments of commerce. Rather, the logic of the marketplace has so thoroughly permeated the consciousness of the business world that it becomes difficult to view a person who is a prospective lucrative customer as a human being first and a business client second. I had many business associates who were also friends, but the acknowledged order of priority was always business first, friendship second.

Rick is a successful trial lawyer who for years plied his trade by doing anything he had to do to win his cases. He agreed that much of his business was to treat people as objects. "I saw people as little pawns in my game and I saw people as being useful to me as opposed to being valuable in their own right."

Like many others, Rick began to question his view of people when he started attending community-building workshops. After sitting for days with others, seeing them pour out their pain and seeing the connections to his own pain, Rick began to change the way he views people:

> **Since going to community building workshops, I have shifted to where I can really relate to people just because they are other human beings, period, without any agenda or desire to get anything back in a material sense.**

Eileen was also someone steeped in the tradition of using people as instruments of commerce. A successful political operative for more than two decades, she suffered a difficult defeat in 1992 when the candidate for U.S. Senate whose campaign she was managing lost the election:

> **I went through a real transformation. I had gotten so caught up in the rat race of raising money, garnering political support, designing ads, attacking opponents, that I really didn't view people as human beings. I saw them as voting units, which were part of coalitions of support that would help us win. It got so intense that I lost sight of who I was and what was really important.**

Eileen went through some deep moments of existential crisis in the weeks and months following the election. In Tillich's terms, one might say she was suffering from acute estrangement from the essential ground of being:

I was lost. I was so deep into the bartering, deal-making system of politicking that, once the campaign was over, I didn't know how to behave. I didn't know what to do.

Then one day, she and her husband were visiting some friends who had adopted two children and their friends described over the course of the evening how much it had changed their lives for the better. As they drove home, Eileen and Jim began to think about adopting a child of their own. Eileen, in particular, felt strangely drawn to this idea and over the next several months, she investigated the possibility. Within one year, they had adopted a little girl, whom they named Carey.

Since then, Eileen has become a so-called stay-at-home mom. People who know her comment that she looks ten years younger and is much more approachable and caring toward her friends. What caused this transformation?

I guess I had lost sight of what it means to be a caring human being. Carey loves us unconditionally and we love her unconditionally. I found what I was looking for and it was as simple as forgetting about all the fake stuff: power, money, fame. Oh, I still think about what would have happened if we had won the election and a part of me still wants that. But it isn't worth the price. Now my biggest thrill is making Carey's lunch and going to her parent-teacher conferences.

What causes people to lose sight of the essential nature of humanity? Why are we so easily sucked into the temporal, existential business of the marketplace? And why do we create such rigid conditions upon which we base friendship and connection with others? Part of it has to do with the search for acceptance. In a marketplace culture, we look for acceptance based on what others think of our performance in the marketplace. Eileen's way of gaining acceptance was to go for the power. "If only I can have enough power over other people, then I will be loved and accepted," we think. The goal becomes so powerful as an attractor that it is easy to lose sight of everything else.

2. The Idolatry of Materialism

Another strategy used to gain acceptance is to surround oneself with prized material possessions and praise from others. If I live in a fancy house with a fancy car and fancy friends, I will be accepted. The paradox is that it is in the striving for such material goods that the goods become the barrier to that which was sought in the first place. Focus on them enough and goods become gods. As Frederick Buechner puts it, in *Wishful Thinking: A Seeker's ABC:*

> Idolatry is the practice of ascribing absolute value to things of relative worth. . .. It is among the non-religious that idolatry is a particular menace. Having ushered God out once and for all through the front door, the unbeliever is under constant temptation to replace him with something spirited through the service entrance.

We need to ask if we are promoting idolatry. A poll of school teachers of baby-boom age (born between 1946 and 1964) asked whether or not their students were significantly different than they themselves had been as kids.

The results of this poll confirm our worst fears about idolatry, particularly in the area of materialism:

Materialism	76%
Anger	51%
Competitiveness	48%
Recklessness	41%

(SOURCE: HORACE MANN EDUCATOR'S CORPORATION, *USA TODAY*, FEBRUARY 4, 1997).

This suggests that 76% of the baby-boom teachers polled feel today's kids are more materialistic than kids were a generation ago. This could be due to the estimated 350,000 television commercials that the average child will watch by the time they turn 18 years of age (Robert Bellah, *The Broken Covenant*).

The idolatry of materialism creates barriers to accepting ourselves and others. Michael Lerner puts it succinctly. In an interview with Peggy Noonan on public television that was aired on February 10, 1995, Lerner was asked how the fact that we are such a secular nation has contributed to the emphasis on materialism:

> People feel the need to fill themselves up for what they experience as lost—and through clever media manipulation and the creation of cultural norms related to consumption, the society helps to shape people who attempt to compensate for this loss through the consumption of goods. It is a futile pursuit because what people are seeking in the way of lost community and purpose can never be compensated for by better cars, fancier houses, or more impressive electronic and computer technologies.

Because we operate in the realm of the known, of that which is concrete and, thanks to the scientific method, that which can be counted and proven, we make gods out of things. The extent to which we can accept ourselves becomes a function of how many goods (gods) we have around us.

This is a clear manifestation of existential estrangement to which Tillich alluded and it has always been present. But in the 1990s, several forces have converged to greatly exacerbate the problem. One such force was the movement of women into the work force.

In the 1990s, almost everyone who is old enough (over 16) is either in the work force or seeks to be in the work force. This is a dramatic change from just 30 years ago when many women stayed home. Apart from the fact that this has been very good for women, the increase in the '60s and '70s in the number of women entering the work force represented as significant a work force change as the industrial revolution. During the industrial revolution, one-third of the work force went from doing one set of tasks (farming) to a different set of tasks (factory work). That same percentage of women entered the work force over the past 30 years.

This change has accelerated the extent to which our society and our interactions with one another have become conditional. When primarily men were making deals in the marketplace, they clearly saw each other as instruments of commerce. But the countervailing force was that they would go home and re-enter a different reality, an environment of acceptance that was usually cultivated by people not involved in the marketplace: women. And there is a yearning on the part of many women in the work force to stay home. A 1990 Gallup poll found that 50% of working mothers would prefer to stay at home if money were not an issue. (Amitae Etzioni, *The Spirit of Community*).

This is not to say that the 1940s and 1950s was an idyllic period by any stretch of the imagination. Many of the interviews in this book reveal thick social masks beneath which families lived in utter misery. Stephanie Coontz, a sociologist from The Evergreen State College has forever dispelled the mythology of the "idyllic" '50s with her brilliant book *The Way We Never Were,* which documents numerous social problems that were actually greater than they are today, but were more effectively covered up.

Nevertheless, women who were not in the work force made their work the building and preserving of what Robert Putnam has called "social capital." The other "product" this work force produced was "unconditional acceptance." The complex networks that women developed among themselves to take care of each other's children have given way to day-care businesses, entities of commerce that professional men and women hire to raise their children while they both go off to work.

Carol was one of the mothers who first stayed at home and now works full time in a demanding, professional job:

I can't honestly say I miss those times, when I was home all day, every day, with the kids. But it is true that the women who were full-time mothers like me led a less complicated life and so did our husbands. Roles were clearer and our neighborhood had a real sense of community. Now that I work full time, I don't know what I would do all day long with my kids.

Women like Carol built networks of friends, exchanged baby-sitting chores by building co-ops, and created places where human connection and acceptance could flourish. The struggle today for everyone in the workplace is that the quest for money becomes all-consuming, so much so that human encounters become a kind of business transaction. This competition further exacerbates the conditional nature of our existence.

3. Zero-Sum Competition

At a recent Community Continuity Conference, a woman from Norway made this observation:

> **I like American men. I am amazed, however, at how driven they are to be successful. And even more amazed that they believe it is important.**

Americans clearly are among the most competitive human beings on earth. And part of what generates this competitiveness is the idea that it is a win-lose or "zero-sum" game. Lester Thurow wrote about this in his 1980 work *The Zero-Sum Society.* The pervasive ethic is born out of a scarcity model: If I don't accumulate, someone else will and there will be no more. This is also a scarcity model in the sense that there can be only one true winner. Thurow defines the zero-sum nature of our existence this way:

> A zero-sum game is any game where losses exactly equal winnings. All sporting events are zero-sum games. For every winner there is a loser, and winners can only exist if losers exist. What the winning gambler wins, the losing gambler must lose.

Peter Senge told a story during a speaking tour in Seattle about how his young son entered a contest sponsored by his school to draw the best Halloween picture. The child spent many hours on the drawing and when the time came for the judges to announce the winner, he was crestfallen to learn that someone else had won. He turned to his dad and said, "You mean, only one person wins?" And his dad had to say, "Sorry son—only one persons wins."

I had a similar experience just this past year when my son ran for the office of vice-president of his sixth grade class. Nicky didn't mount much of a campaign like the other kids. They had fliers with slogans like "Don't be mean, vote for Dean" and "Don't be a pain, vote for Jane." Some kids tried to buy the election by bringing huge jars full of candy and putting "Vote for Billy" on the outside of the jar of candy.

The day of the election, I was driving Nick to school and he said, "What am I going to do about the election, Dad? I have to give a speech, but I don't know what to say." So we devised a speech that would play on his creative and acting skills. He decided to go up to the podium in front of the class and say, "I am not very good at speech making and I really wouldn't know what to say anyway. But I brought three people with me who have some things to say. He then went over and came back as Forrest Gump and did an endorsement of his candidacy imitating the voice of Gump. Then he went back and did the same thing with Peppy Lepeau and Astro the Space Dog: "Re Rove Rou Rick."

After all was said and done, Nick and another candidate tied for first place in the election. They had a run-off election and his opponent won by one vote. Nick took it in stride, but I confess that coming from the zero-sum culture and being extremely competitive, I found myself saying, "What could we have done to push him over the top?" I realized how ruthlessly "conditional" this system is for kids. There is one winner and the others are losers. And it is only the unusual kid who would put him or herself through such a process again. Such kids become politicians.

The zero-sum conditional culture is pervasive. If you don't believe it, try to remember who the losing presidential candidates were for the past, say, four elections. Or, try to remember who came in second in the Olympic decathlon in 1996. One of the best signs of this phenomenon is to look in the "people" or

"Hollywood stars" sections of magazines. Typically you will see a list of "Who's Hot and Who's Not," or "Who's In and Who's Out." All of this oozes with conditionality and the effect it has on us is to treat each other and ourselves conditionally. Nothing is more destructive to the building of trust than to participate with others in a system in which, if you don't beat them, they will beat you, "you will lose."

It should be little wonder that the number of people who say they trust their fellow man has dropped from 58% in 1960 to 37% in 1993. If virtually every encounter we have is with someone in the context of the marketplace who can either help us or hurt us, and they are thinking the same thing about us, why should we trust anyone? In *Following Christ in a Consumer Society,* John Kavanough summarized one perspective of the consumer culture in which we live:

> I know of no other force so pervasive, so strong, and so seductive as the consumer ideology of capitalism and its fascination for endless accumulation, extended working hours, the drumming up of novel need-fulfillments, the theologizing of the mall, the touting of economic comparison, the craving for legitimacy through money and possessions, and unrelieved competition at every level of life.

In my own work, the zero-sum competition has played itself out for real. After all, as my son has learned at an early age, elections are "winner-take-all" and I found I was willing to be fairly nasty in order to avoid losing. And the winner-take-all system is, as ES has said, "a game you can't win." In politics, if you lose, you are "a loser." If you win, you are beholden to the voters who will burn you in effigy at the slightest provocation.

In business, if one makes money the sole goal, it, too, is a game you can't win. If you don't end up with millions of dollars, you are considered (or you consider yourself) a failure. If you do end up with millions of dollars, you begin to suspect your friends' motivations and you find it difficult to trust either friends or colleagues.

The most dramatic example of this is the state lottery winner whose life has been literally ruined by his winning five-million dollars several years ago. Since becoming an instant millionaire, his wife has left him and sued him for her share of the money, his brother tried to kill him so he could inherit the money and the winner himself has totally isolated himself and has no friends because he trusts no one. This particular "winner" has been so devastated by his money that he recently asked the state to take the money back! Since no one has ever asked them to take the money back, the state is currently trying to figure out if they can do that.

4. Image Perfection

One of the biggest barriers to acceptance is the preoccupation people have with narrow definitions of perfection. It is a truism that there are ideal forms the marketplace promotes daily: images of beautiful, thin, rich men and women fill the newsstands, television shows and now the Internet.

Our culture focuses on perfection so much that we have come to idolize those who appear to be close to becoming the "perfect" fighter or the "perfect" actor. Some even refer to scripture as a justification for the focus on being perfect. When we look in the scripture, we do, in fact, find at least 47 references to the word "perfect" or "perfection." One of the more famous examples in the New Testament is in Matthew 5:48:

Be perfect, therefore, as your heavenly Father is perfect.

But Greek scholars will tell you that the Greek word for "perfect" is *teleios,* which actually means "to be complete." Therefore, when we read about the call to perfection as noted in scripture, it is not meant to be a call to what the culture means by perfect, as in "without blemish" or "flawless" (meaning skinny, rich and successful). Rather, it is more accurately a call to be complete or whole. We are simply called to completion.

Harold Kushner, in his book *How Good Do We Have To Be?*, addresses this same point. He says that in Genesis 17:1, God said to Abraham, "Come and walk with me and be tamim." The Hebrew word *tamin* has been translated variously as "perfect" or "blameless," suggesting that we are indeed called to be perfect. But, says Kushner, more contemporary scholars have taken the word to mean something more along the lines of "whole-hearted" or "whole." Kushner says:

> My own study of the verse leads me to conclude that what God wants from Abraham, and by implication from us, is not perfection but integrity. God wants Abraham to strive to be true to the core of who he is, even if he strays from that core occasionally. . .. As Mother Teresa once told an interviewer, "We are not here to be successful; we are here to be faithful," which I take to mean faithful to our essential selves as well as to God.

But in the clutter and noise of capitalism, such subtle distinctions, although of vital and profound significance to the way we live, often are lost.

As noted previously, a typical American child will watch 350,000 television commercials by the time he or she turns 18. This bombardment of images into the consciousness of Americans has a numbing, but persuasive effect.

The effect of such image promotion is that anyone who doesn't stack up against such images is "less than." This results in what Michael Lerner and others have called "self-blame." As described in Chapter Three, scientific studies of patients in psychotherapy show that, before therapy, there is a dramatic gap between their perceived self and their ideal self. After therapy, the patient sees that they are not as bad as they had thought; they have changed their view of themselves.

Self-blame is often the primary cause of this initial gap. It is the internalizing of thousands of negative messages about oneself that result from feeling "less than" compared to the images that pervade our culture. Combine this with the zero-sum nature of competition and the result is often acute anxiety and depression.

This gap between perceived and ideal self closes through the healing power of acceptance, which helps individuals become aware that they have blurred the reality of their self images, making them out to be far worse than is true. Thus the culture of conditional love invades the way we think about ourselves, and self-love and self-acceptance becomes conditional.

In our study of workshop participants, we asked people to report how they felt before and after the workshop in a number of areas relating to self-acceptance and authenticity. For example, we asked: "How important is accepting yourself for who you are?" The participants described a significant change from before the workshop to later:

IMPORTANCE OF ACCEPTING YOURSELF: (*% answering "Very"*)	Before	Now
The importance of accepting yourself for who you are	57%	87%

The average change was 52.6% between before the workshop and later, when the participants took the survey. We believe this reflects the power of unconditional acceptance. Group therapy is designed to create a space where the whole individual is unconditionally accepted for who they are. Exposure to such pure and unconditional acceptance, even briefly, as with a three-day workshop, can begin to show people what it would be like to practice unconditional acceptance in the real world.

5. The Outer-Directed Person

Sociologist David Reisman first coined the terms *inner-directed* and *outer-directed* in *The Lonely Crowd,* in the 1960s. He used the terms to describe the change that American culture brought about as a result of the industrial revolution. He explained that prior to the industrial revolution, man was more inner-directed because he gained self-esteem and acceptance primarily from conquering the challenges of nature, which required inner strength and fortitude. The industrial revolution saw man beginning to gain acceptance by exploring and exploiting his interaction with others. Self-esteem and acceptance, at least for men, was transformed from inner- to outer-directed as a result of being able to use the force of one's personality to win people over: customers, other businesses, employees. But this shift has contributed to the barriers to self-acceptance since it is not particularly clear in the 1990s how one should act in order to gain acceptance.

Another question we asked was: "How important are the opinions of others to you?" The answers again reflect fairly dramatic changes:

IMPORTANCE OF THE OPINIONS OF OTHERS: *(% Answering "Very" or "Fairly")*	Before	Now
The importance of the opinions of others	81%	48%

A decline of 42% in the importance of the opinions of others is dramatic and, when taken together with increases in the importance of self-acceptance, it suggests that self-acceptance and inner-directedness go hand-in-hand. The literature on the effects of group therapy clearly shows that one of the positive effects experienced by participants is that of becoming more inner-directed. As far back as 1951, Carl Rogers cites this finding in his work *Client-Centered Therapy* and he calls it a shift from having an "external locus of evaluation" to an "internal locus of evaluation."

Why is this an important shift? The more reliant I am on others for acceptance and love, the less grounded I feel because the approval of others is so fleeting in nature. And since we live in a society of conditional love, if most or all of my sense of self comes from others, I will spend most of my life trying to meet the elaborate conditions often laid out for me, in order to gain such approval.

Melissa explains how her reliance on the opinions of others affected her:

Before the workshop, the importance of the opinions of others was huge for me. If someone didn't like me, I was devastated. I always thought, "What did I do wrong"? I used to take everything personally. I could turn anything around and blame myself for it.

Now I feel, if people don't want to take the time to get to know the true me—not just the me they initially perceive—then they are missing out on a cool person.

Marty, a mother of four who has attended many community-building workshops, puts it this way:

One of the ways workshops have changed the way I am is that before, I was externally motivated. I always did things for others, never really considering what I, myself, wanted. Now, most of the time, I ask myself "What do I want? What do I need?" I know that what is best for me is best for all concerned, because I won't feel resentment. I just take care of myself, and that's the only person I can do a good job taking care of, anyway.

Marty makes a profound point here. The paradox of community-building is that it helps people become fully separate and independent of others, which then helps them be free to connect.

M. Scott Peck makes this point in *The Road Less Traveled,* in the section called "Love and Separateness":

> A major characteristic of genuine love is that the distinction between oneself and the other is always main-

> tained and preserved. The genuine lover always perceives the beloved as someone who has a totally separate identity. Moreover, the genuine lover always respects and even encourages this separateness and the unique individuality of the beloved. Failure to perceive and respect this separateness is extremely common, however, and the cause of much mental illness and unnecessary suffering.

Separateness is a condition of genuine connection and should be established even before committing to a relationship, according to Sam Keen. In a lecture several years ago, Keen recounted a conversation he had with Howard Thurman, a colleague whose opinion he greatly respected. Thurman told him:

> There are two things you must figure out as you enter maturity: You must decide where you are going and who might go with you—and if you ever get those two things in the wrong order, you are in big trouble.

In our society, we learn to depend on the opinions of others for our worth and a sense of who we are. In so doing, we can become enmeshed in the random and fleeting opinions others have of us, resulting once again in the image of a cork bobbing in the ocean. The antidote to such insecurity is to look inside oneself for direction and meaning.

Mihaly Csikszentmihalyi, in his book about optimal experience entitled *Flow,* put it this way:

> There is no question that to survive, and especially to survive in a complex society, it is necessary to work for external goals and to postpone immediate gratifica-

> tions. But a person does not have to be turned into a puppet jerked about by social controls. The solution is to gradually become free of societal rewards and learn how to substitute for them rewards that are under one's own powers. This is not to say that we should abandon every goal endorsed by society; rather, it means that, in addition to or instead of the goals others use to bribe us with, we develop a set of our own.

The barrier many of us have to moving toward inner-direction is that we think others will not like us because we are not necessarily doing what they want us to do, and because we live in such a conditional-love culture. But the paradox is that, while on a surface level others might be annoyed by one's independence and inner-direction, they often admire individuals who appear to have the courage to act based on a clear, strong and independent sense of where they are going.

Conclusion

Perhaps the single biggest barrier to authentic connection and acceptance is the conditional-love basis of the culture in which we live. The quid pro quo nature of trade and commerce, the tendency for human beings to idolize material possessions, the zero-sum nature of competition, the unrealistic expectations we place on ourselves to achieve the perfect image and the excessive reliance on the opinions of others all combine to make it difficult for people to accept themselves, much less others.

Community building can counter the forces that move people away from feeling connected, and help them move toward self-acceptance and peace, as we shall see in coming chapters.

Recommended Reading:

Buechner, Frederick. 1973. *Wishful Thinking: A Seeker's ABC.* San Francisco: HarperSanFrancisco.

Coontz, Stephanie. 1992. *The Way We Never Were.* New York: Basic Books

Etzioni, Amitai. 1993. *The Spirit of Community: The Reinvention of American Society.* New York: Simon & Schuster.

Kavanough, John F. 1981. *Following Christ in a Consumer Society.* Maryknoll, N.Y,: Orbis Books.

Kushner, Harold. 1996. *How Good Do We Have To Be?: A New Understanding of Guilt and Forgiveness.* New York: Little, Brown & Company.

Lerner, Michael. 1996. *The Politics of Meaning: Restoring Hope and Possibility in an Age of Cynicism.* Reading, Ma.: Addison-Wesley Publishing.

Meyers, David. 1992. *The Pursuit of Happiness.* New York: Avon Books.

Reisman, David. 1961. *The Lonely Crowd.* New Haven: Yale Press.

Thurow, Lester. 1980. *The Zero-Sum Society.* New York: Basic Books.

Chapter Five

Social Masks and the Authentic Self

From childhood on, first our family and then our culture are the mirrors in which we see ourselves as acceptable or not. When we need to conform in order to be acceptable, we may end up wearing a false face and playing an empty role if who we are inside and what is expected of us are far apart.

—Jean Shinoda Bolen (Gods in Everyman)

You're only one person. If you try to be anybody else but that person, it's just not going to work. You don't have to have autism to understand that. That works for everybody.

—Jerry Newport
(A man with autism, interview, "60 Minutes," Sept. 29, 1996)

How does the individual come to learn to hide their truth, their authentic feelings, emotions and behaviors? When do they come to learn that which is acceptable and that which is unacceptable? One description of how this happens comes from

Robert Bly in his work *A Little Book on the Human Shadow.* Bly says:

> When we were one or two years old, we had what we might visualize as a 360-degree personality. Energy radiated out from all parts of our body and all parts of our psyche. A child running is a living globe of energy. We had a ball of energy all right; but one day we noticed that our parents didn't like certain parts of that ball. They said things like, "Can't you be still?" or, "It isn't nice to try and kill your brother." Behind us, each of us has an invisible bag, and the part of us our parents don't like, we put in the bag, to keep our parents' love.

Bly's image of the 360-degree personality emphasizes that human beings were born with the capacity for all kinds of behavior. Over time, however, in an ongoing effort to be accepted, we slice off certain kinds of behavior that those around us see as unacceptable and we put it in what Bly calls a "bag" and what Jung called the "shadow." These behaviors are stored in our unconscious. As Jung says:

> Everyone carries a shadow, and the less it is embodied in the individual's conscious life, the blacker and denser it gets. If an inferiority is conscious, one always has a chance to correct it. But if it is repressed and isolated from consciousness, it never gets corrected, and is liable to burst forth suddenly in a moment of unawareness." (Storr, *The Essential Jung*).

The shadow part of our personality can become extensive if we learn growing up that the way to become accepted is to please others. Authentic behavior such as crying when one is hurt, or laughing when one is happy, can be hidden to the extent such behavior is unacceptable. When it is unacceptable, it is covered up and the resulting behavior becomes part of something called the "persona." The word persona comes from the Latin per sonare, "to sound through," and it was, according to Jung, originally used to refer to the mask worn by actors to indicate the role they played.

For our purposes here, the persona is a social mask that each individual uses to get love and acceptance. It can take any number of forms, and one of the exercises that often is part of the community-building workshop is to draw one's own social mask. The purpose behind identifying the masks people wear is not necessarily to convince them to discard their masks but, rather, to discover the existence of masks and to begin to discover what may lie in the shadow or "bag" part of one's personality.

The social mask people wear may also be considered a protective shield from the waves of judgment and criticism floating around in our culture. Telemarketing salespeople for example, are trained to assume a persona that is different from themselves, so that when 98 out of 100 people they call hang up or swear at them, they do not feel personally rejected. In the same way, many people, whether consciously or unconsciously, assume certain kinds of behaviors in order to protect themselves from the harsh realities of the ocean of judgment in which we live.

Another way in which the social mask is manifesting itself is on the Internet. Chat rooms abound in cyberspace, which makes it possible for individuals to communicate with one another anonymously, making it even more possible to assume a false identify while interacting with others. In addition, numerous studies have strongly established that 55% of communication cues are visual, 38% are vocal (sound) and only 7% are verbal (words). Thus, in a chat room conversation, with just 7% of the full communication available, along with the possibility that someone might be concealing all or part of the truth, one wonders how such relationships will play out in the future.

Jane is a successful social worker who freely acknowledges that she wore a mask of perfection for much of her life. She had a lot to say about the role of social masks in her life:

I was an only child and I was reared to be the perfect little princess and a perfectionist. I was reared with conditional love: The message was, "If you don't do what I want you to do, I won't love you." So I got love and acceptance by putting on the social mask of perfection. Since I was treated this way, I treated others the same way. I couldn't do things wrong—because they didn't think I could do things wrong. And so I hid all those imperfections and in the process I also hid them from myself.

The effect of doing this is great. People have told me over and over—and I used to be proud of this, although now it appalls me—"You've got your life together—you are one of those people I can look at and say, "Oh, this is how I want to be." I used to respond to that by thinking it was cool. Now I would think, "Oh my God, if you only knew the truth." I am able to be more transparent now. The community-building workshop really pointed out that I can do that and not die. It is an exercise in having faith in myself, to do that.

The big fear was always that people would find out what I really was like. When I can say that I hurt, I bleed, I'm lonely, I find it bridges the gap between me and others, instead of creating a gap. It's the mask—the defenses—that creates the gaps between me and other people.

So, the workshop allowed me to lower my mask. It also brought into conscious awareness for me my own pain and that of other people. When I don't look at my own pain, then I can't look at others' pain. I can be very good at blocking out pain.

When you are perfect, that, of course, means others are not. I was very condescending. This "air" of superiority masked the great feeling of inferiority, the doubts that I felt as a child that I would never name. I had a full scholarship to a prestigious, private university in Tennessee and I wouldn't go because I didn't feel I could measure up—I knew the truth about myself. But I wouldn't tell anybody why. So I went to a public university and my excuse was that my S.A.T. scores were high, so I could waive freshman English if I went to the public university, and I hated English. I was able to mask my fear of failing at the private university. I didn't want to be hurt, and the perfection mask was an armor against pain.

I've always tried to walk a tight rope, keeping everyone happy and accepting of me, through "perfection." Then about ten years ago I decided I didn't have the energy to do this anymore. I always had known there had to be a different way. I set out on a voyage of self-discovery. I did a lot of reading, I got into therapy. I had just run out of steam—it was depression that had not been diagnosed. I just couldn't give anymore.

I have had to learn to be a receiver. There's a lot of grace in being able to receive from people. I was more of a giver because I thought I could better control my feeling of being wounded. This kept the mask intact: "Oh, what a giver, what a wonderful woman." And all the time I was dying inside. So, to be able to be authentic now means sometimes you get to see the rotten side of me.

I realize that my first obligation is to myself and to be authentic. I know that the only way that love and acceptance

can grow is when I am authentic with others. Real love can only happen in an authentic situation. And I mean real love, not just warm feelings. Love is an act of will, an act of intentional acknowledgment for the other.

On the last day of my workshop, a woman from South Africa handed out some cards, one to each participant, each with a different word. I looked at mine and cried because it had the word "forgiveness," with a little picture of a person kneeling at the feet of another. I had picked the right card. The most difficult task for me is to forgive myself and to forgive others. When I can do that for me, then it just flows like a river to other people.

Being gentle with myself is something very new. Before, whenever I would do something wrong, I would rant and rave at myself. When I catch myself doing it now, I laugh and say, "Oh, lighten up--you are being too hard on yourself." It's not that I no longer have that reaction, but I am quicker to recognize it and put things into perspective.

Part of the reason we wear social masks is to avoid judgment from others in a world of conditional love. Unfortunately, the thicker the mask, the more estranged we become from our authentic selves. This estrangement creates barriers to connecting with others and accepting oneself.

Heather wore a number of different masks throughout her childhood and into her early 20s. She learned very early on that it was not okay to make mistakes and that if you did, you would be publicly shamed for it. As she reached the age of puberty, Heather noticed that she was not as interested in boys as the other fifth-grade girls. She asked her mom about it and her mom said, "Oh, don't worry, Honey, I wasn't interested in boys at your age either. Give it time."

Then something happened that changed her life forever. One day after school, Heather came home and saw what looked like her *Weekly Reader*, in a plain brown envelope. It was addressed to her and so she opened it. To her shock, it was a magazine for lesbians and it had a picture on the cover of two women embracing.

When her mom got home, she showed her mom the magazine and said "This is what I've been talking about, Mom." Her mother said, "Where did you get this magazine, young lady?" and she abruptly took it and threw it away. Heather never did figure out why or how that magazine came to her house, but she did learn something about herself—or at least she had been given a clue, much as I had been given clues about having been adopted, although I had not picked up on them.

Heather recognized by the time she went to high school that she was gay, but she very effectively covered it up with the mask of "over-achiever, perfectionist." She continued to wear different masks over the years, all related to the need to compensate for her "shameful" secret .

In her late 20s, Heather entered a master's program that focused on hospice care for the dying:

> **Working with death brought up existential thoughts. For example, the idea of freedom: If I am really free, why am I living with all these restrictions just because the outside world says it's no good. And the notion of "meaning": "What meaning will my life have if I continue to live this lie?"**
>
> **I started to visit with people who were dying and I asked them what their regrets were. Almost all of the regrets were about relationships: time with people, wishing they had been more authentic in their relationships. Those talks hit me hard.**

Heather subsequently decided to "come out" and let the world know she was gay, and she became a powerful voice on behalf of AIDS victims in the early 1980s. While she still struggles to remove her well-developed and widely varied social masks, she has no regrets about being openly gay and living authentically:

The freedom of not hiding things about myself from people is tremendously liberating. I would never wish on anyone what I went through to cover up reality.

The ability to remove one's social mask begins with a willingness to accept oneself. In Heather's case, she had to get to the point of accepting being gay before she could open herself up to the judgmental world. With therapy and a great support system around her, Heather found the courage to truly be who she is, something that we believe people are called upon to do.

Yet we, each of us, in the culture of conditional love, struggle with these differences and with our willingness to risk being authentic, especially if it means being different. It is much easier to blend in, to "go with the flow." And many people do not want to reveal authentic pain and struggle, for fear of being judged. But British poet David Whyte (*The Poetry of Self-Compassion.* Audiotape. [Langley, Wa.: Many Rivers Company]) points out that the soul is not interested in such superficial distinctions:

> The tendency is to refuse to confront one half of our existence, the dark side: what's difficult about our lives, what's grief-filled about our lives, what's painful about

> our lives, what's flawed about our lives. And the hope is that you can just concentrate on this other side and everything will be marvelous and good. And all the time, one side of it is just atrophied.
>
> And the soul doesn't seem to make the distinction between the light and the dark. It chooses both. It doesn't care whether you do something successfully or fail at it. It just wants to know "did you do it in your way?" Was it you who failed or were you trying to be someone else when you failed? If it was you, the soul's happy. That was your experience, your failure, no one can take it away from you.

The social mask can be a barrier to identifying authentic emotions and feelings that have been repressed. The amount of judgment a person encounters during the course of just one day might be enough to preclude them from ever removing their mask, and the difficulty is that the more the mask is worn, the less likely a person is to identify what is really going on for them.

The human organism essentially uses the social mask as a defense mechanism against other people's judgment. The goal of the therapeutic relationship is to create a safe environment to help the individual get in touch with those previously hidden emotions, and integrate them into awareness. This also is precisely the goal of the community-building workshop process.

In our study of participants, we wanted to know how the workshop may have impacted their ability to remove their social masks. We asked: "How comfortable are you removing your social masks with the following people?":

COMFORTABLE REMOVING MASK

(% Answering "Very" or "Fairly")

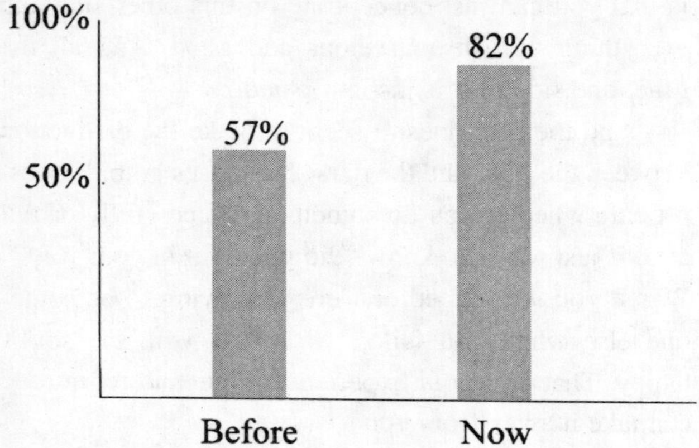

This represents a 43% increase in the number of participants who felt "Very" or "Fairly" comfortable removing their mask. (SOURCE: 1996 COMMUNITY BUILDING STUDY)

Moving from an average of 57 percent to 82 percent represents a 43% increase. Why the dramatic improvement? What did the experience of sitting with people and listening to their stories do to make individuals so much more willing to drop their social masks with others outside the circle? The implication once again is that the group experience through this model makes people willing to risk being authentic no matter what the cost.

There is a deep yearning to be authentic with one another and workshops provide a kind of laboratory where it is safe to experiment. Once people have a taste of what it is like to be authentic and be accepted for it, they want to continue to be authentic.

Of particular interest was the finding that people continued to feel comfortable removing their social mask after significant time had passed, even after two years. This suggests that the benefits to participation in community building may be ongoing. The differences in willingness to lower the social mask depending on who a person is interacting with is another interesting element of these findings. (See Appendix A.)

It bears repeating that the healing that can come from acceptance in groups leads to autonomy, to the feeling that one is free to do, act, think or feel what one chooses. But if I don't accept myself, I will continue to cover up my sense of inadequacy with social masks and close myself off to others.

The trends toward social isolation and disconnection described in Chapter Two may well be driven by the dynamics of repressing authentic emotions, putting up false fronts and placing conditions upon relationships in the pursuit of material wealth.

Until we choose to disengage for significant periods of time from these cultural forces and nourish our relationships with ourselves and with others, we will continue to be isolated from each other. Janice Barfield, one of FCE's co-founders and a 15-year veteran of facilitating community-building workshops underscored the way self-acceptance precedes acceptance of others:

> **I find it important to have "community" within myself. As I experience more community within my own self, then I will feel more community with other people. The more I get into community within myself, the less I care about what others think of me. It is really self-acceptance and when I am in touch with myself and with my higher power, I feel freer to be with other people.**

Janice's point is verified by survey data. We posed the following question to workshop participants:

One of the assumptions underlying the community-building workshops is that many people experience a gap between who they are and how they feel deep inside (the authentic self), versus how they believe they must act in order to get along in the world (the social self), a concept Carl Rogers has called "incongruency."

How would you have rated yourself in terms of the congruency between how you felt (authentic self) and how you acted (social self) immediately before attending the community building workshop, compared to now? Were you very congruent, fairly congruent, not very congruent or not at all congruent with the following individuals?

CONGRUENCE

(% Answering "Very" or "Fairly")

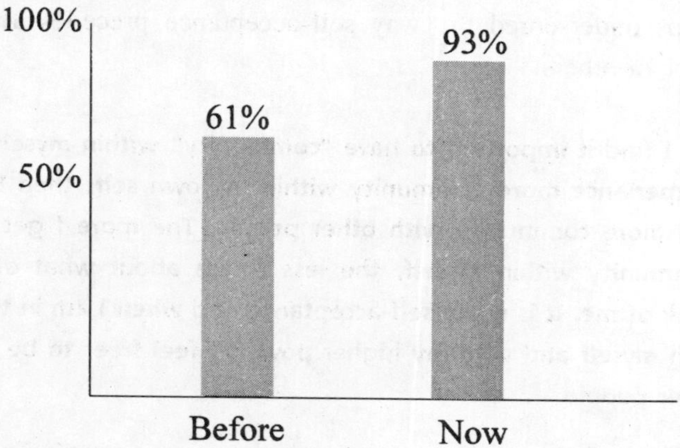

This represents a 53% increase in the number of participants who replied "Very" or "Fairly" to the question, "How congruent do you feel?" (SOURCE: 1996 COMMUNITY BUILDING STUDY)

Once again, there were dramatic improvements in the extent to which individuals felt they were being more congruent or authentic in relation to others.

Contemporaneous with feeling more self-accepting, better able to lower one's social mask and less dependent on the opinion of others, participants also reported that they felt more connected to various people in their lives as a result of community building. We asked: "How connected did you feel to the following individuals before the workshop and now?":

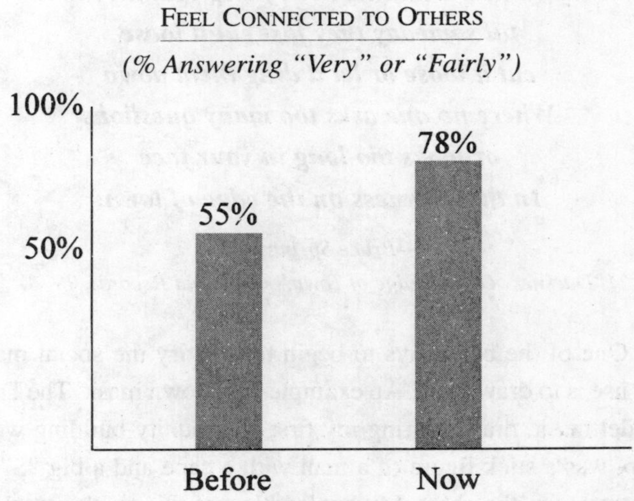

This represents a 41% increase in the number of participants who replied "Very" or "Fairly" to the question, "Do you feel connected to others?" (SOURCE: 1996 COMMUNITY BUILDING STUDY)

This increase in the number of participants who reported feeling more connected with others is extremely significant because it suggests that there is a relationship between acting authentically and connecting with others. As one participant put it, "Taking risks and sharing authentically is the essence of effective communication in relationships." The paradox is that we avoid relating authentically out of fear of rejection or judgment, yet when we muster the courage to do it, it helps to connect us more closely with other people.

Exercise: Draw Your Mask

Everybody's got a secret, Sonny
something they just can't face
Some folks spend their whole lives trying to keep it
they carry it with them ev'ry step that they take
till someday they just cut it loose
cut it loose or let it drag them down
Where no one asks too many questions
or looks too long in your face
In the darkness on the edge of town.

—Bruce Springsteen
("Darkness On the Edge of Town," Columbia Records, 1978)

One of the best ways to begin to identify the social masks you use is to draw them. An example is my own mask. The Doug Shadel mask, drawn during my first community-building workshop, was a stick figure of a man with a cape and a big "S" for Superman on the chest. My explanation of this mask was that I hide behind the persona of always being in charge and always being in control. Prior to the workshop, I had never heard of the idea of social masks and it was helpful to become aware of times when I wore it and times when I felt safe removing it.

Bill's social mask is a face with glasses and a pipe. He uses the "I am a really super-reflective intellectual" mask.

You will recall Jane, who wore the mask of perfection: "The social mask for me was: not a hair out of place, perfect makeup, a smile and always right," she says. The social mask of perfection is very common at workshops and it has a lot to do with the image-perfection concept discussed in Chapter Four. In order for us to get what we need, love and acceptance, we feel we must follow the proscribed rules and come as close as we possibly can to the images promoted by the popular culture. Little wonder that Americans spend billion of dollars per year on plastic surgery, hair-replacement surgery, and diet books, tapes and programs.

It is a peculiar irony that a nation known for its rugged individualism becomes a nation of groupies, all following the winds of cultural trend to gain acceptance and identity, only to all end up looking fairly similar. Philip Slater made this point in his book *The Pursuit of Loneliness:*

> Many societies exert far more pressure on the individual to mold herself to play a sharply defined role in a total group pattern, but there is variation among these circumscribed roles. Our society gives more leeway to the individual to pursue her own ends, but since the culture defines what is worthy and desirable, everyone tends, independently but monotonously, to pursue the same things in the same way. Thus cooperation produces variety, while competition generates uniformity.

Now it's time for you to draw your mask(s). On a separate sheet of paper, you may want to write down thoughts you have about this mask. Remember, that a lot of people use more than one mask. As you think about it, you can use the following questions as guidelines:

1. How often do I wear this mask?
2. Why do I wear it?
3. In what situations am I likely to wear this mask?

4. When do I feel most comfortable removing it?
5. What happens to me during those times when I have removed my mask(s)? And, am I being more authentic?

A final thought about social masks. We are not suggesting that one should at all times and at any cost remove their social masks, revealing the authentic self and one's true emotions. There are many times when it is not only appropriate but also necessary to wear social masks of various kinds in order to operate in the world. But the key point is to be aware of when you are wearing the mask and when you are removing it. As one participant said after a workshop where she learned about her mask or, as she put it, her "wall":

The single most important thing that I learned from community building is that I recognize the walls that I have built up to protect myself. I didn't realize what a steel-reinforced, cement-upon-steel-upon-bricks-upon-steel wall I have. I drew my social mask: shoot you with daggers, don't look at me wrong, your "best defense is a good offense"—you know. I have comebacks for everything. That was the biggest realization for me and to realize everybody has their own wall—some may be plastic, some may be brick, but you realize that everybody has their own little world, their own difficulties. I realized that the "woe is me" isn't going to work, because everybody's in the same boat—just at different levels.

Once I was able to identify the wall, I find that I am able to drop it more often and it is very scary. Sometimes I will pull three bricks down and then I put five on top. The first two days of my workshop, the wall came down and then, for some reason, on the third day somebody said something to me and the wall went back up. At least I was able to recognize that. I

began to be aware of the wall. It took me 32 years to see the wall—I never knew it was even there. Now I feel we are working together.

It's useful to consider your mask to be an ally or a tool that you can work together with to cope with the harsh realities of modern life in the '90s.

Recommended Reading:

Bly, Robert. 1988. *A Little Book on the Human Shadow.* San Francisco: HarperSanFrancisco.

Bolen, Jean Shinoda. 1989. *Gods in Everyman.* New York: Harper & Row, Publishers.

Hopcke, Robert. 1995. *Persona: Where Sacred Meets Profane.* Boston: Shambhala.

Parry, Alan, and Dolan, Robert E. 1994. *Story Re-Visions: Narrative Therapy in the Postmodern World.* New York: The Guilford Press.

Slater, Philip. 1970. *The Pursuit of Loneliness: American Culture at the Breaking Point.* Boston: Beacon Press.

Chapter Six

The Self-Blame/Judgment System

It is often tragic to see how blatantly a man bungles his own life and the lives of others yet remains totally incapable of seeing how much the whole tragedy originates in himself, and how he continually feeds it and keeps it going. Not consciously, of course— for consciously he is engaged in bewailing and cursing a faithless world that recedes further and further into the distance. Rather, it is an unconscious factor which spins the illusions that veil his world. And what is being spun is a cocoon, which in the end will completely envelope him.

—Carl Jung

WHAT CARL JUNG IS, OF COURSE, REFERRING TO IN THIS PASSAGE is the concept of psychological defenses, which people use, as we have seen in the last chapter, to protect themselves from the harsh attacks of a judgmental world. We have suggested that the trick to overcoming the negative effects of psychological defenses like social masks is awareness: If people can only become aware of when they use masks, they can begin to get a handle on the effects.

Likewise, it is crucially important to begin to understand the way different psychological phenomenon relate to and impact on each other. To integrate into our awareness the complex web of psychological phenomenon that can impact an individual, we must begin with the concept of systems thinking.

Peter Senge describes the systematic nature of the universe this way in his classic work *The Fifth Discipline:*

> A cloud masses, the sky darkens, leaves twist upward, and we know that it will rain. We also know that after the storm, the runoff will feed into groundwater miles away, and the sky will grow clear by tomorrow. All these events are distant in time and space, and yet they are all connected within the same pattern. Each has an influence on the rest, an influence that is usually hidden from view. You can only understand the system of a rainstorm by contemplating the whole, not any individual part of the pattern.
>
> Business and other human endeavors are also systems. They, too, are bound by invisible fabrics of interrelated actions, which often take years to fully play out their effects on each other. Since we are part of that lacework ourselves, it's doubly hard to see the whole pattern of change. Instead we tend to focus on snapshots of isolated parts of the system, and wonder why our deepest problems never seem to get solved.

The systems approach is a recognition of the interconnected nature of reality. The mystics have a saying that even a butterfly in Beijing flapping its wings affects the course of events.

Just as seemingly disparate, separate events like clouds forming and ground water flowing are interconnected, so, too, can be seemingly unrelated psychological phenomenon within human beings. One such phenomenon is the self-blame/judgment system and it can be a major barrier to acceptance and connection. The self-blame/judgment system can be described as follows:

> In a culture of conditional love and harsh judgment, the individual mercilessly internalizes such criticism and blames himself in response. This causes him to employee the strategy of judging others so that, by comparison, he will feel better about himself. The individuals he judges, however, also internalize it and blame themselves and they, too, respond by blaming others.

The first question to ask is why people are so self-critical. One possible explanation comes from the role of "stories" in defining who we are. In *Leading Minds,* Howard Gardner talks about the way stories can help leaders lead: "I argue that the story is a basic human cognitive form . . . stories speak to both parts of the human mind—its reason and emotion. It is stories of identity—narratives that help individuals think about and feel who they are, where they come from and where they are headed—that constitute the single most powerful weapon in the leader's literary arsenal."

Stories are also the principle way we begin to determine how we stack up in comparison to others. There are cultural stories that create a context or backdrop for how we are doing compared to everybody else. One of the most predominant "stories" of our time is the preoccupation with success and wealth. This is a story that says to the individual in response to his question "Am I acceptable?": "You are if you make a lot of money."

Madison Avenue, with its dominant influence on the images that filter into the homes of hundreds of millions of Americans each night, has really controlled the story around which we evaluate who we are. Most often, in comparison to the thin models or the business tycoons that dominant the media, we come up lacking.

The psychological response to this feeling of not stacking up to the predominant cultural messages is self-blame for failing to compare favorably to the images of perfection. Self-blame leads to judgment of others, which in turn leads to being judged by those same others.

One can begin to see the cyclical, self-perpetuating nature of this system rather quickly. Could it be that part of the reason we live in such a harshly judgmental society is that so many individuals have internalized so much of the negativism floating around in our culture that a critical mass of us simply do not like ourselves and are on a search-and-destroy mission to pull down anyone in sight, which, by so doing, makes us feel marginally respectable in comparison?

In interview after interview, we heard people outline the cycle of self-blame followed by the judgment of others to make themselves feel better.

George is a 42-year-old, divorced step-father of two who started going to community-building workshops in 1992. He explains his own experience with the self-blame and judgment:

For me, the basics of judging come from self-hate. The pain will go away as long as I can judge other people to be bigger schmucks than I am. I am a schmuck, but they are bigger schmucks than I am, so I am okay. The judgment and self-blame began for me with my dad. My dad was probably one of the most powerful agents in my psychological development and for years, I judged him to be less than I needed him to be and to

be uncaring, because I looked at this man and said, "He's bright, he's capable, why can't he change himself to be what I need him to be, why couldn't he have done that for me." I judged him and in the process, I judged myself, mercilessly.

I judged myself because I never measured up to his standards. I could never get his approval, so I thought he saw me as unacceptable, and my interpretation was that I was unacceptable.

This was the way I would think and when I really experienced problems, when I was self-medicating with alcohol, ultimately, I would get angry at everybody else for being failures. You know, "My step-kids can't apply themselves and can't follow the rules. And my wife can't hold them to the rules. She doesn't have enough strength to do it, she doesn't have enough motivation." So I judged everyone. It was safe because I didn't have to confront the reality that I was a mess, too, so I judged myself to be better.

The blaming helped me put the problem elsewhere. One of the most profound impacts of the workshop for me was that when I talked, I had 25 people listening. And that was both frightening and wonderful. It was as if some of the energy of the universe was being focused on me. I guess part of the reason for me being able to go out into the world and not blame and judge others so much is a sense that I have already experienced unconditional love from a large group of people.

The emptying we did helped me to stop judging myself. Because the more I empty my own stuff, the more I come to understand how similar I am to every other human being. I see how broken I am and how this connects me to every other human being. It's a wonder any of us can function at all. I don't know if I got to the point of saying, "Boy, we really need to help each other," but I did come to realize that my judging insulates me, it disconnects me from my fellow human being.

For those of us who were and may continue to be outer-directed people, meaning we seek and require approval from others, such apparent disapproval may result in playing the "I'm better than you are" game, which is what George is describing when he says he viewed others as "bigger schmucks than I was."

Rick, who we heard from in Chapter Four, also saw the self-blame/judgment mechanism play out in his relationships with others:

I used to think anything anyone did was stupid if it wasn't as smart as what I would do, and that meant a lot of people were stupid. I don't know where it came from—societal conditioning, probably. People are making judgments all the time. I suppose it derives from insecurity. You know, I have to be one up or one down. That's what it is. It's a particularly male tendency to be one up or one down with people, and if you make a judgment against someone, you're one up.

Tony was a macho biker who was arrested in 1985 for battering his girlfriend. The courts gave him a choice: he could either go to jail for three years, or go into a program known as a "responsibility" group. He chose the group. This group met twice a week for two years and if Tony missed even one session without requesting permission, he would be sent off to jail. All of the participants in the group were batterers who had received deferred sentencing like Tony.

Tony says he would come into the meeting and the therapist would say, "How was your day today, Tony?" Tony would immediately start blaming his rotten day (and his rotten life) on his girlfriend, Pam. "I came home and the stupid broad hadn't cleaned up, dinner was late, and she was in a bitchy mood."

The therapist would then say, "Tony, what percentage of your bad day was Pam's fault? He would say that 99% of it was her fault. The therapist would then say, "So, the other 1% was your responsibility? "Yeah, I guess so." "Great, then let's focus on that 1%."

The goal was to help the person stop hiding from their own self-blame by blaming and judging others. After years of therapy, Tony now realizes what he was doing:

I blamed others so I wouldn't have to face the fact that I felt worthless. When they would tell me to take responsibility for my actions, I would see just how low my own self-esteem was. Since I have been to therapy, my whole family has started going, too. And after years of hiding the facts from me, my dad recently came to me at the suggestion of his therapist and told me he had raped my sisters over a period of years. I don't know if that contributed to my self-blame and hate, but I'm pretty sure it explains why my dad was so distant from me and my mom. And all this time, I thought he just didn't like me.

M. Scott Peck, who has written extensively about the process of growing up and becoming mature, is very big on the idea of taking responsibility of one's own life. In *The Road Less Traveled & Beyond,* he says:

> . . . what most characterizes immature people is that they sit around complaining that life doesn't meet their demands. On the other hand, what characterizes those relative few who are fully mature is that they regard it as their responsibility—even as an opportunity—to meet life's demands.

Now that we have reviewed the self-blame/judgment system from the perspective of Tony, let's hear from a woman who was married to a person like Tony. Melissa is an employee of Carlisle Motors, the car dealership that has sent 500 of its employees through community-building workshops. In an interview, she described the enormous personal growth and insights she gained from the workshop, and, in so doing, she discussed the self-blame/judgment system of which she was both a victim and a perpetrator:

I am very critical of people and I am very judgmental of people and I do not trust anyone—I have zero trust. It's because I was raped at age 14 and this eliminated the trust factor for me. I shared that information with the group and it clicked with a lot of people; they said, "Oh, okay." I don't use it as an excuse or as a crutch, but it never leaves you.

My being able to share that helped me see that I could trust that group of people. To say it in the privacy of your house or with a good friend is one thing, but to say it to complete strangers in a room full of people, knowing the owner of the company you work for is sitting right there, was scary. But it also was a relief for me to be able to say, "Let me explain myself a little bit—maybe if you see this side of me you will understand me more. You start with a preconceived notion of who people are and, later, you begin to see the softer side of them.

I blame a lot of my being judgmental on my parents' prejudices. Both my mom and dad are judgmental. To them, everybody has a classification. People are not just people, they are "something," and I viewed people this way all my life.

I was trying to find fault in everyone else to make myself feel better. "They are just as bad as I am. They screwed up,

too. Good!" I was trying to make myself feel good by finding fault in other people, to make me look not so bad in my own eyes.

Now I'm not as hard on myself as I used to be. I had gone through a divorce, a child-custody battle, nine years of a humiliating marriage and my self-esteem was nil. Through the workshop and through my present husband, my self-esteem has slowly been built back up. So I am more accepting of my faults. That doesn't mean they are permanent. I know I can change, I know I can work on it and just recognizing the faults, and recognizing that the defense mechanisms are there, is a huge step.

My former husband blamed me for everything. It was his defense mechanism. Part of being able to accept myself was realizing his blaming me was more about himself than it was about me. I saw this during the workshop when we did an exercise about how defenses work. We were drawing a person on a big sheet of paper, and I remember one of the other gentlemen in our group said, "draw a pointing finger." That was his thing. He said it was so much easier for him to point at other people than to point at himself.

And when I heard him say that, it was like hearing the slot machines in Las Vegas when you win: Ding-ding-ding-ding-ding! I had been blaming myself for everything that went wrong in the marriage and this insight just lifted that weight off me.

Someone later on said something that was also a mind-blowing insight. She was saying, "I don't have any problem with confrontation because I take care of myself first. If someone is making me miserable, I have to let them know they are making me miserable; otherwise, I am not taking care of myself." Suddenly she saw what she had been doing. "All this time, I've been trying to fix everybody else instead of fixing myself," she said. So a big insight for me was to accept others' opinions and my own, and if they disagree, to accept the differences instead of one of us trying to convert the other.

I find that the less I blame myself, the less I judge others— it's just that simple. And the more accepting I am of myself, the more accepting I am of others. It's such a simple thing— we all went to Sunday school and learned to do unto others as you would have them do unto you. Why didn't I listen? All these years, it would have made life so much easier if I had practiced that.

My friends have seen the change in me and even my parents have seen the change. I have said more to my parents in the past two years than I have said in the previous 33 years. I have been more honest with them, more direct with them, more emotional, more free with my feelings. It's been very positive.

My father is in the hospital right now recovering very well from surgery and when I visited him, for probably only the seventh time in my life I said, "I love you" to him. And I didn't even think twice about saying it. Whenever I see him now I say, "I love you," and he looks at me as if I were not his child, because that's something my family just didn't say. Now he says he loves me, too, and I think, "Isn't it silly that we didn't do that all the time?"

I feel much more connected to them than I ever have. I look at people differently now. "You can't tell a book by its cover;" hear their story first. I am more open-minded now. I saw so many sides of people, people I would have formed an image of, just based on their appearance. Was I wrong. I realized I wasn't seeing them at all.

Your confidence in the people and your doubt about them are closely related to your self-confidence and your self-doubt.

—*Kahlil Gibran (*Spiritual Sayings of Kahlil Gibran. *The Citadel Press, 1962.)*

Judgment and blame is pervasive in our culture because so few people have been able to avoid the self-blame/judgment cycle. Michael Lerner thinks the Rush Limbaugh / Hot Talk radio phenomenon in the early 1990s was the result of white middle-class males getting caught in this system of self-blame and projection of blame and judgment onto others. His theory, articulated in a book entitled *The Politics of Meaning* is that after years of being blamed for oppressing blacks, women, the poor and so forth, white middle-class males have internalized such blame into their unconscious and it is now being projected outward on Hot Talk radio. The key reason for this projection of anger is that the white, middle-class suburban folks don't have it so hot, either:

> Follow the lives of many suburban-dwelling corporate types as they assemble early in the morning on trains and buses or on crowded freeways, making their way to work, from which they will return exhausted and depleted . . . follow them as they spend each day learning how to treat others as objects, and internalizing the message of the market: that we must look at one another from the standpoint of what we can get from other people, not from the standpoint of their being embodiments of God. Watch them as they become migrant laborers, moving around the country at the behest of corporate sponsors or in search of a better job . . . watch

> them as their marriages fall apart, their children rebel, their neighbors don't know them and their co-workers seek ways to best them in the marketplace . . .. Sure, many corporate workers have more options than do others . . . [but] even those who seem relatively privileged are often themselves in real pain.

The pain we all face is exacerbated by the significant barriers that prevent individuals from relating deeply and authentically.

In our study of workshop participants, we asked people to rate various "significant barriers" to connecting with others before the workshop and now. Here is a list of the top barriers reported and the extent to which they changed:

SIGNIFICANT BARRIERS

(% Answering "Very" or "Fairly")

	Before	Now
Hard to find people you can trust	65%	32%
Fear of being judged	61%	13%
Fear of being rejected	55%	10%
Feeling misunderstood	52%	16%
Unable to lower my defenses (social mask)	48%	0%
Too shy	42%	21%
Fear of appearing weak	35%	7%
No opportunity to meet people interested in connecting	30%	16%
Average	48%	13%

Notice that fear of being judged or rejected were the second and third most frequently mentioned barriers to connecting with others. Perhaps even more interesting was that these two barriers were among those most greatly reduced by participation in the workshop.

The supposition we make and which many, many participants made in interviews is that the barriers to connecting with others directly relate to one's own insecurity and lack of self-acceptance. Then people learn they can change. The door is acceptance.

One of the principle ways in which workshops help people gain self-acceptance is that they get clear pictures of others as opposed to the distorted marketplace images of perfection and success. The self-blame/judgment system is set into motion by cultural and marketplace images.

THE SELF-BLAME/JUDGMENT SYSTEM

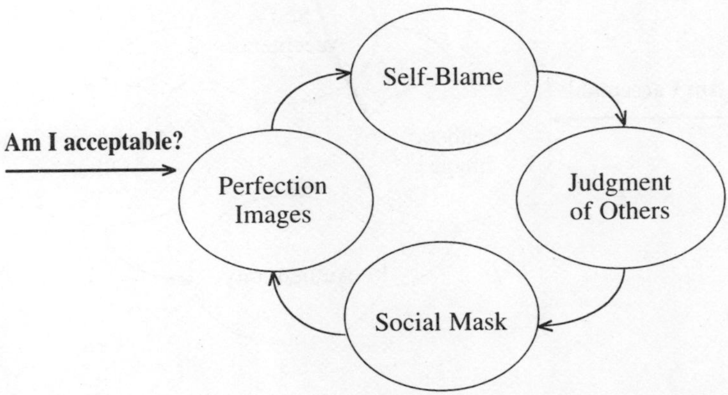

In this first diagram, we show the system beginning with the individual asking the question "Am I acceptable?" As we mentioned at the outset of this chapter, many psychologists today believe that our sense of identity or sense of self is often determined by how we position ourselves in relation to the cultural stories we internalize. Therefore, in trying to answer the question "Am I acceptable?," we look to our relationship with the images that abound about success and what it means to be "acceptable" based on the cultural story of the day.

You can see by the first diagram above that the self-blame/judgment system can lead from the self-blame that results from concluding that, compared to the standards of the marketplace, I am "less than" worthy and therefore not acceptable, to judging others in order to feel more acceptable, to wearing social masks to avoid being judged, which in turn leads to a perpetuation of the false images projected by the marketplace.

THE SELF-ACCEPTANCE/AUTHENTICITY SYSTEM

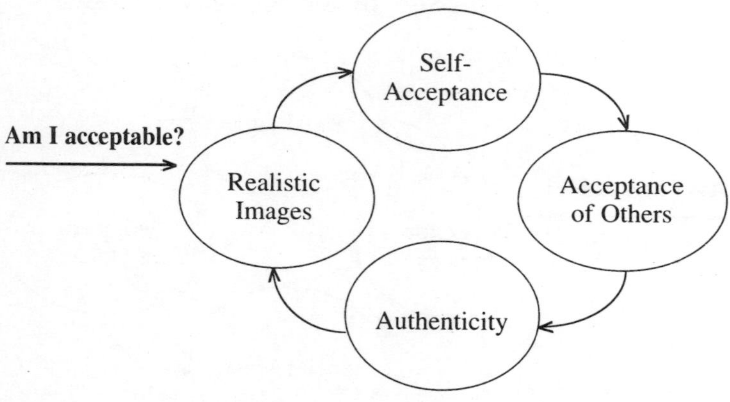

In contrast, this second diagram shows the self-acceptance/authenticity system. This system can be set into motion by participation in community-building workshops or other support groups that encourage authentic storytelling to help people accept themselves. This works because the "stories" are real and people see that they are just as good as most others; such self-acceptance can then lead to accepting others, since acceptance of self has been pretty clearly established as a precondition to accepting others, which itself can lead to living authentically.

Obviously these two different systems or paths are not always followed in precisely the manner described, but in our extensive interviews with people and analysis of the study findings, the patterns were significant enough to compel us to offer this observation.

Cindy is yet another example of a person who fell into the self-blame/judgment system. She felt unaccepted as a child and consequently blamed herself for somehow not being worthy:

I was trying hard to be perfect because I felt so imperfect—my father didn't chose to have a relationship with me after my mother and he divorced. I found I held myself and other people up to extremely high standards because I felt inadequate inside because my dad didn't want me. I was trying to make myself into somebody that he wanted and I pushed that standard onto everybody else. It made me kind of unpleasant to be around.

Something about hearing other people's stories made Cindy realize the self-blame/judgment cycle she had become stuck in and she changed:

I benefitted tremendously. Hearing a person's story made a huge difference. I became able to acknowledge the positives in people, and less willing to make a judgment about the negatives.

Cindy also realized that she was not the only one who had suffered rejection in her life. Hearing about other people's rejections helped her realize rejection is not always about her, but could be about the person doing the rejecting.

Hearing other people's stories of rejection made me realize that my father not being in my life doesn't make me less of a person. I have all these wonderful qualities and his rejection wasn't because of me—he doesn't even know me.

This is a powerful insight because fear of rejection is a major barrier to connecting with others. Clearly Cindy is not alone in having the workshop help her accept herself and others and reduce the fear of rejection. Our study showed a whopping 81.8% reduction in participants' fear of rejection before the workshop versus later (see Appendix A). In addition, participants reported a similar reduction in their fear of being judged (78.7%).

These phenomena have been noticeable to me in my own experiences with the community-building workshop. I remember just basking in the freedom to be accepted (or not judged) and in the immediate aftermath of a workshop, I was far more accepting of others than I had been before. There is a direct correlation between feeling good about myself and accepting others. When I have just achieved something I'm proud of, I want to connect with others, and I want to connect with others because I don't need to judge them to build myself up.

Conversely, when I am feeling like I have not done well or I blame myself for this or that, I can literally see a change in my outlook toward other people. I get a hardness to my view and I look for things to judge about people in order to feel better, something that all four of the individuals mentioned in this chapter have observed about themselves. As George says, "I am a schmuck, but there are bigger schmucks than I am, so I'm okay."

The self-blame/judgment system is yet another manifestation of the estrangement we experience in our existential world from the essence from which we came.

Having lost sight of our being unconditionally accepted creatures, awash in a judgmental, conditional world in which we evaluate our worth based on what those outside of us think (outer-directed), we quickly internalize judgment and then turn around and judge others as a survival mechanism. The antidote to this is acceptance.

FEAR OF BEING JUDGED

(% Answering "Very" or "Fairly")

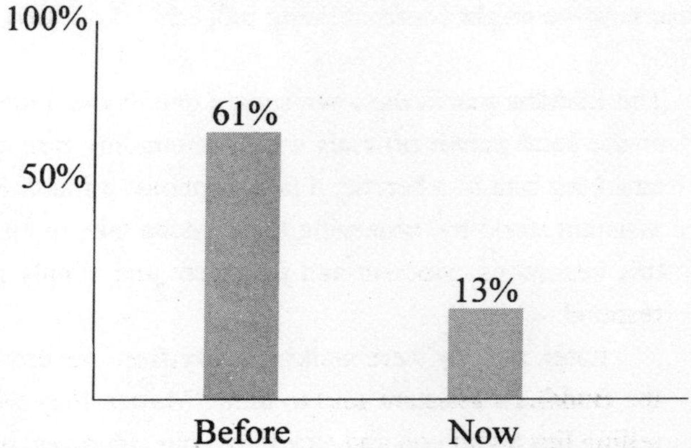

This represents a 79% decrease in the number of participants who replied "Very" or "Fairly" to the question, "Do you fear being judged?" (SOURCE: 1996 COMMUNITY BUILDING STUDY)

Webster's has several definitions of "judge," including "to pass judgment" or "to decide authoritatively," but the one I found most interesting was definition four, "to have as an assumption or to suppose."

This definition resonates with me because one of the main things I have learned during the course of my involvement with community building is that it is virtually impossible to see the world exactly as any other human being sees it. We are all vastly different in terms of our families of origin, our experiences and even our particular biological composition. Yet so much of the time we assume we know what another is feeling, thinking or seeing.

So, the judgments I make about people are really nothing more than a series of assumptions about who they are, what they mean and how they feel. And if this is true of the judgments I make about others, the judgments others make about me are also assumptions which may or may not be true.

There is a story about the Buddha that makes the point about how we might confront being judged:

> The Buddha was in the town square one day and many of the local public officials were surrounding him and attacking him as a heretic, a fake, a phony, a fraud. His assistant stood by, observing the Buddha take in all of this venomous criticism and judgment and simply not respond.
>
> Later, as they were walking away from the crowd, the Buddha's assistant said to him, "Master, they were telling lies about you and attacking your character; why didn't you defend yourself?" The Buddha thought for a moment and then said, "Let me ask you a question. If someone gives you a gift and you choose not to accept it, to whom does the gift belong?"
>
> The assistant said, "To the giver?"
>
> The Buddha smiled and continued walking.

The single most profound point I have learned from community building is that much of the judgment I have experienced in my life is less about me and more about "the giver" of the gift of judgment. This is not to say that I have never been deserving of judgment or criticism; I have. But the challenge is to discern what is legitimate criticism and judgment, which I can use to grow, and what should be discarded as an unuseful and even potentially damaging "gift."

One might use Peck's distinction between existential fear and neurotic fear. Existential fear, says Peck, is when you are walking in the jungle and you see a lion charging toward you, so you decide to run. In this instance, your fear comes from the primal instinct to survive. And because the lion looks like he will eat you and, in fact, WILL eat you if you don't run, you run. Neurotic fear is when we begin thinking the entire world is out to get us, and they are unreal or unrealistic anxieties.

It is just possible that the same distinction could be made for self-blame and judgment: there is both existential self-blame and neurotic self-blame. The former arises when I have done something that really will hinder my growth as an individual or the growth of another. The latter, neurotic self-blame, is when we begin to introject or internalize all of the comments around us that even remotely resemble negative evaluations of us, and even some that are not directed at us that we internalize anyway. The goal of therapy then, whether in a group or individually, is to help the person clarify what is existential self-blame and what is neurotic self-blame.

The significant barriers to individuals connecting have a lot to do with how aware we are of our own self-blame/judgment system and that of others. I will probably never eliminate the extent to which I blame myself and internalize the criticism of myself from others and then project it outward, but becoming aware of these processes has helped me to accept them and therefore minimize their effects. That which we can feel, we can heal.

ES says there are two kinds of people in the world: people with pain who know it and people with pain who don't know it. Those with pain who don't know it are most susceptible to becoming a captive of the self-blame/judgment cycle because they are less aware that it is a dynamic presence in their lives.

Consider the following interaction between Tony, the batterer we discussed above, and his girlfriend, Pam, which he described in interviews with us:

Tony: **(to Pam) "You are such a lazy bum. The dishes aren't washed, the bed hasn't been made and you look like a wreck."**

Pam: **Why do you always criticize me? I work all day, too. I am doing the best I can. I got a raise today at work.**

Tony: **A raise? For what? For doing your job? Give me a break!**

Pam: **Look, I bought a new dress today. Do you like it?**

Tony: **With whose money? Not my money, damn it—take it back. Besides, it makes you look fat.**

By Tony's own admission, each one of these attacks on Pam was merely a reflection of his own self-blame and insecurity. Tony was insecure about his own personal hygiene (he often would go days without bathing or shaving), so he projects those insecurities out onto her:

I basically shoved every insecurity I had about myself onto my girlfriend. I didn't like it when she got a raise because I was unemployed; I didn't like it when she bought a new dress because I blow money like water going down a drain, so I criticized her for that. I learned from therapy that the things I hate

most about people are the things I hate most about myself. That has been a huge insight.

There is always a danger in analyzing the way projection works in people because it is a complex phenomenon. Thousands of scholarly articles and studies have been done about it. The amazing thing about the examples we have cited here, particular Tony's, is that his analysis of what was happening with self-blame, judgment and projection was his own accounting, guided by years of therapy.

The self-blame/judgment system is a major barrier to acceptance and connection. One of the most effective ways to reduce judgment is to begin to accept oneself—both the good and the bad. As Nathaniel Branden has said:

There is overwhelming evidence that the higher the level of self-esteem (self-acceptance), the more likely one will treat others with respect, kindness and generosity. People who do not experience self-love have little or no capacity to love others.

Exercise: Identify Your Shadow

This exercise is designed to help you identify those aspects of yourself that you have repressed into your unconscious and dislike either intuitively or because of social pressure.

Think of someone you simply cannot stand. Picture the person clearly in your mind. Now take a pen and paper and list the five things you despise the most about this person.

Once you have written this list, read over the characteristics that drive you crazy about that individual. These are the shadow parts of yourself, the areas which cause you to engage in self-blame.

Conclusion

Until more people begin to remove their social masks and bring into awareness both the light and the dark, we will continue the self-blame/judgment system along with all of its consequences.

By surfacing previously stuffed emotions and feelings, projection of negative self-images is minimized and the "cocoon" that Jung describes, quoted at the beginning of this chapter, begins to unravel, revealing a wondrous human being waiting to be released from the bonds of self-blame and self-doubt.

Recommended Reading:

Abt, Lawrence and Bellak, Leopold, eds. 1950. *Projective Psychology: Clinical Approaches to the Total Personality.* New York: Alfred A. Knopf.

Branden, Nathaniel. 1994. *The Six Pillars of Self-Esteem.* New York: Bantam Books.

Ferris, Anthony, ed. 1962. *Spiritual Sayings of Kahlil Gibran.* New York: The Citadel Press.

Gardner, Howard and Laskin, Emma. 1996. *Leading Minds: An Anatomy of Leadership.* New York: Basic Books.

Lerner, Michael. 1986. *Surplus Powerlessness.* Reading, Ma.: Addison-Wesley Publishing Company.

Peck, M. Scott. 1997. *The Road Less Traveled & Beyond.* New York: Simon & Schuster.

Sahakian, William S. 1974. *Psychology of Personality: Readings in Theory.* New York: Rand McNally & Company.

Storr, Anthony. 1983. *The Essential Jung.* Princeton: Princeton University Press.

SECTION THREE

Islands of Acceptance

CHAPTER SEVEN

Individual Transformation

You enter the forest at the darkest point
where there is no path.
Where there is a way or path,
it is someone else's path.
You are not on your own path.
If you follow someone else's way,
you are not going to realize your potential.

—Joseph Campbell

BILL THATCHER: THROUGHOUT THIS BOOK, WE HAVE MADE references to our study of community-building workshops and the impact the Foundation for Community Encouragement (FCE) model of community building has had in the lives of individuals. We have provided some of the results from our formal research findings to anchor the anecdotal stories from individuals about their experience with the culture of conditional love, social masks and the self-blame/judgment system. While the research findings speak to the rational side, the stories speak to the soul.

In this chapter, we provide a thumbnail sketch of the model itself and the theoretical underpinnings upon which it is based in order to create the context for our discussion of community building in a number of different settings. It will also provide a helpful context for the rather lengthy but fascinating story that ends this chapter: the diary of a community-building participant.

The community building model most closely resembles the marathon groups described in research by American psychologist Carl Rogers and Stanford researcher Irving Yalom. In Chapter Three, we trace the study of groups over the past fifty years and provide our explanation of where this model fits.

While Dr. M. Scott Peck was central to the establishment, more than twelve years ago, of the FCE and to the model's introduction and development, there have been scores of other people who have contributed to its success. The model continues to undergo change and refinement even though Dr. Peck retired from the board of FCE several years ago.

The FCE model seems to have a consistent pattern of success. It works relatively quickly, does not require success by every participant for there to be group success, and it uses group learning rather than a lecture approach to enhance learner retention.

The theoretical framework for this model is very much in the tradition of the leaderless marathon group and client-centered therapy as defined by Carl Rogers. Rogers outlined three conditions in which healing can take place either in a group setting or one-on-one with a patient. The three conditions Rogers describes are:

1. Unconditional positive regard
2. Congruence
3. Empathy

1. Unconditional Positive Regard

This is the condition of unconditional acceptance, which is a pre-condition to individuals feeling free (sometimes for the first time in their lives) to lower their social masks and look inside for authentic feelings and emotions. Rogers, when asked how he can unconditionally accept individuals, some of whom he may dislike, said that it is not the individual's behavior at the moment that he focuses on. Rather, it is the acceptance of where that individual is at the moment and the potential for improvement that resides in everyone, that he can accept.

The community-building workshop, with its rules of "no judging, no fixing" and the instruction to speak in the first person, facilitates the creation of an environment of the unconditional positive regard to which Rogers alludes in describing the optimal therapeutic environment. This may explain in part why so many participants report improvements in their ability to remove their social masks and a reduction in the fear of being judged or rejected.

2. Congruence

Congruence is simply another word for authenticity. Rogers defines it as alignment between authentic feelings and emotions (authentic self) and the way we behave in order to get along in the world (social self). In order for healing to flourish in a group, the leaders or in the case of the FCE model, the facilitators, must model congruency or authenticity. The goal is to encourage participants to feel free to experience and express their authentic selves as much as possible.

In Chapter Five, we reviewed the research on how participation in community building improved an individual's ability to live more congruently in relation to others. Rogers and many others in the field of psychology believe that living congruently, or authentically, is a primary factor in psychological growth and healing.

3. Empathy

This characteristic of the optimal healing environment is a bit harder to pin down precisely. For lack of a better way to put it, the goal is to create an environment in which all of the members of the group, while listening to another member, attempt as much as possible to put themselves in the other's shoes and experience their reality with empathy and respect. In community building, this really plays itself out in the form of empathetic listening.

The operating assumption of Rogers's theory and the FCE community-building model is this:

> The human organism naturally moves in the direction of healing and wholeness, but barriers in the form of judgment and self-blame can block such movement. The creation of a judgment-free environment helps to remove the barriers to this natural process, thereby allowing the individual to heal him or herself.

Often participants will become frustrated that the facilitators don't say much and, seemingly, don't do much throughout the first two days of sitting in a circle. We will hear more from these facilitators, but for now, suffice it to say that there is a solid theoretical rationale for leaderless groups. Simply put, the model operates on the firmly held assumption that the individual is the only person who can heal him or herself—a therapist can't do it, a guru can't do it, a book can't do it and furthermore, a facilitator may get in the way of healing because the participant can come to depend on someone else or something else doing it for them.

This may sound dangerously close to the rugged individualism that we have so thoroughly trashed, although it is not. While individuals must heal themselves, this can only be done in the context of others creating the kind of space necessary to accomplish it.

The FCE model facilitates the creation of such a safe place, an environment in which the conditions are optimal for individuals to help each other heal themselves.

Thousands of people, in many countries of the world, have been through this community-building model. But the FCE and the model face a significant challenge if it hopes to expand in the future. For one thing, the model is most often thought of as an isolated event where learning can occur, and once the event is over, its over. In order to have a more lasting effect, the model must be adopted more as a set of principles than as an event fixed in time. While the model "feels" like an event for most participants (and an exhausting one at that!), it offers a doorway into a life process. The building of community in this way is more analogous to traveling on a road than reaching a destination.

The model is more principle-driven than structure-driven and this can be unsettling for someone looking for the "one right way." There are certainly structures present that facilitate the application of the principles such as unconditional positive regard, congruence and empathy (and others). But these can be moved or added as the group requires. It is in this sense a dynamic model.

One structural example is having people sit in a circle. There are many reasons why this chair arrangement can be helpful but if the circle gets in the way of community building, it can be changed. The model does not say, "You must be in a circle for community to occur." It would be sad if that were the only way for community building to be possible, because most of our life is lived outside of a circle!

The challenge to groups seeking to use this model in continuing community environments is that reverberations from its use extend throughout their entire organizational structure and life. We examine this aspect when we describe the impact one organization, Carlisle Motors, has experienced in using this model.

Next is a description of my own first experience with the FCE model and then we share with you the "diary" of a person who attended their first community-building workshop in July, 1996.

The first FCE community-building workshop I attended as a participant was a facilitator-training workshop in Knoxville, Tennessee. The only preparation I had was from reading Scotty's book where he describes the stages a group goes through: pseudo-community, chaos, emptiness, and community. From reading the book I thought I had a good grasp of the concepts. I was wrong. The first two days I had no idea what stage the group was in at any given time!

Scotty was one of the two facilitators for our group. In getting things started he presented some ground rules for our time together. One rule he mentioned was for each one of us to speak when we were moved to speak and to not speak when we were not moved to speak. Through the entire workshop I was never moved to speak. This was disturbing to me. I had never sat in a group for so long and said absolutely nothing! It wasn't that I was withdrawn from the group. In fact, a couple of people mentioned toward the end of the workshop that they were aware I hadn't spoken but had felt I was fully engaged as a participant. Since for so much of my adult life I have made my living in jobs where speaking forms an important part of what I do, silence in the group was a new and helpful—though totally unexpected—experience for me.

Over the course of the workshop there was a great deal of emotion expressed in that room. I was unprepared for the strength and the depth of emotion. There was much pain shared.

At the conclusion of the first day I could not see how we would move into anything even approaching a sense of community by the end of the workshop; but we did.

When the workshop was over, I left feeling confused. I had gone to Knoxville for answers and come home with more questions. This was not, I decided, going to be an easy process. I reread parts of *The Different Drum* and spoke on the phone with Scotty and others about my experience.

Several months later I returned to Knoxville for my second facilitators' workshop. This time I approached it differently. I didn't try to understand anything. I put aside my questions and tried to be fully present. As I began to experience the process I also began to understand. By not trying to figure out where the group was in the process, I felt free to follow the process wherever it went.

The linear description of the stages of community building in Scotty's book had caused me to think that one stage followed another. Not necessarily so. The image I have now is of a staggered-start race with sixty runners (I realize a sixty-lane oval track has not been built but, hey, it's my image). Everyone started at a different point around the track. As we "ran," the distance between us kept changing. Some would sprint ahead. Others would pace themselves differently and even drop behind. But most of us ended in a bunched-up group at the end.

Even though development continues on this community-building model there are several distinctive characteristics that are central to its identity.

When we were planning the research for this book, we considered and then discarded the idea of tape-recording a community-building workshop. There were problems with that idea. What we didn't consider was asking someone to keep a diary. Imagine our surprise when just such a "diary" appeared from Norway on our fax machine during the final month of writing the book. The twenty-four-year-old person who sent it has given us permission to use it here.

Diary of a Participant

My name is Kaarstad. I have a confession and I hope you will take it quite seriously. Three years ago, I would have sneered contemptuously if anyone had told me that I willingly would attend a sit-in-a-circle-and-cry-on-each-other's-shoulders group. You see, ever since I was little, I've despised groups like that. Now and then I would see them on television, and every time, I would snort loudly and promise myself I would never be seen in such a group.

"What's with these people," I would say to myself. "Don't they have any friends they can turn to? Don't they have any sense of dignity? How can they be so weak? And in public! How can they stand to show their emotions to complete strangers? For Pete's sake! It's pathetic, it's shallow and it's not something I would ever do!" For years, I repeated this litany at every opportunity, and generally thought it uplifting to nurture my pet-hatred to new heights. After all, who could it harm?

There came a time when I happened to have to spend a very long time in bed with a half-destroyed ankle, some nerve-wracking books and my own dubious thoughts for company. Among the things I came to confront during this time was my long-standing hatred for groups of the community-building kind. There are many things I dislike, but why had I bothered to drive this particular dislike into flaming hatred? Only gradually and with a great deal of ill will did I come to the conclusion that I hated such groups because the thought of ever attending one of them terrified me. I have always been a private person, and I'm not keen on sharing my inner thoughts.

So, I was frightened, and often, when I discover I'm frightened of something, I feel a wild urge to try it out. Not that I'll go parachuting off a mountaintop just because I'm afraid to, but I have made a hobby of tumbling toe first into any opportunity to confront my inner fears.

More than a year and a half passed before I actually attended such a group. This was partly because of a tight schedule, but mostly because I needed the time to consider. North America is quite a trip from Norway, and I wanted to be as certain as possible that this was what I wanted to do with my money. One thing is dashing about, being spiritually courageous, another thing is being practical where money is concerned.

One of the reasons I eventually chose to go was that the FCC, which was the alternative in question, seemed delightfully practical in its orientation. If there is a way to change groups from being overly polite and inane into rational, efficient units one might talk to, I wanted to know about it.

To that end, I went to the FCE's Ninth Annual Community Continuity Conference, held near Toronto in 1996, and the following are my subjective impressions from that conference, some of which were written on the spot, and some later. This is not a full account of what happened at the CCC. I have tried to confine myself to my own inner experiences, preferably those stemming from things that happened in my small group.

Barrie, Ontario. Wednesday, July 24, 1996.
Registration day.

I came in early today to have ample time to fret over the forthcoming business. To keep myself calm, I went about reconnoitering the grounds. It's hot here compared to home, and even the water in the large lake is warm. The pine trees are different. Knife and fork are placed on the "wrong" side of the dishes.

Details like that are amusing, but they remind me I'm going to be one of the odd ones out here. Oh, I know that the others will probably be doing their best to make me feel comfortable, but I worry about the subtle, invisible cultural differences that none of us will be aware of until they've caused trouble.

What's more, I worry that people will see uncommon aspects of my culture as uncommon aspects of my specific personality, and set about trying to make me more acceptable in their eyes. It saddens me to think that what I consider valuable might be interpreted wrongly or—worse still—never taken into account at all. It's so easy to forget that I'm Norwegian, or that that could cause a cultural clash. People notice that I speak British English, but they don't notice that I have to think long and hard to remember to add "please" when I ask for something. People notice that I don't know the current political issues in their country, but they don't notice that many of the references they use only come naturally to natives. Take "Star Trek," or, "The Wizard of Oz." Most Norwegians would stare blankly if you said, "Beam me up, Scotty!" or talked about a yellow brick road.

I was pondering these matters and trying to assure myself that I was unduly concerned, when a fellow a little ways off suddenly waved his arms at me and bellowed: "How are you?" I stopped dead in my tracks and looked at him, shocked. What was wrong? Why had he raised his voice at me? Was I trespassing?

Then the meaning of his words filtered through, and my instant desire was: "Who are you, stranger? How can you ask such a personal question?" I finally decided that, "I'm fine, thank you" would be the more appropriate reply. By then the poor chap had been standing about looking hapless—and all for trying to be friendly. I decided to escape indoors.

My greatest concern is that I don't have any idea of what's going to happen. Of course I've come armed with knowledge of what's supposed to happen and what might happen, but

unique human beings are such an unpredictable lot. What am I doing here anyway? I don't even like groups. They so often insist on doing the wrong thing.

Going on this adventure is like boarding a ride with a sign by the entrance that says:

Constructor's Notice
Welcome to the magical community ride!
New and amazing roller-coaster technology
has enabled us to present you with this
Truly Unique Experience!
(Should there be any problems,
please don't hesitate to fix them yourself.
We don't really know more about
what's going to happen than you do.)
Thank you

At least I find the people here friendly and easy to talk to. They are generally curious and eagerly supply me with cultural information at the slightest provocation. I felt unnerved to find that almost everyone I meet here are old pros at community building. It's natural that they would be, what with this being a community-continuity conference, but somehow I'd never given it a second thought. Now I'm painfully aware that I'm as wet behind the ears as a newborn fish, and surrounded by strangers who for the most part already know each other. It scares the living daylights out of me. Theoretically. If I were to admit to such a feeling.

Being a solitary person, I am a little astonished at how much I've been speaking with people today, and how much I've liked it and felt understood. And this is before we've started. It

leaves me thinking: "Well, look how we all smile today. We'll probably be furious with each other by tomorrow afternoon."

The two most commonly asked questions here are: 1) What brought you here? And 2) What are your expectations?

What brought me here: I used to work at a bookseller, and that's how I came across Peck's books. This community-building thing seems like a good idea, if it works, so I came because I'm curious. As for my expectations—oh, I don't really know. I'll just hang around and see what happens.

That's what I say. Here's what I think.

First of all, I expected this place to be filled with wishy-washy people—mostly single women with eyes brimming with tears; people who would speak about nothing but "sensitively growing." But, in fact, there seem to be as many men as women, and there are several couples. Also, the personal stories I've heard so far are more stout than wishy-washy. To my great relief, no one has as yet talked about beans, yoga or being sensitive.

Second, I expect that if I open my mouth during the sessions, I'll make an utter fool of myself and regret it for the rest of my life. Therefore, I have every intention of behaving like a slightly dead oyster. A slightly dead listening oyster.

Thirdly, I expect everyone to sit around and grin sheepishly for the first couple of hours in the group. Then I expect we'll start hurling insults at each other. As the anger gathers momentum, we'll grab each other by the throats and try to strangle one another. Or, we'll all sit staring dully into the air, trying to remember why we came here. And that's all that happens.

Actually, what I really think, is: We'll reach "community" in no time, and live as happily as we possibly can ever after, or at least until the conference is over.

Barrie, Ontario. Thursday, July 25, 1996. First day.

If Jesus Christ were to come today, people would not crucify Him. They would ask Him to dinner and hear what He had to say, and make fun of it.

—Thomas Carlyle (1796-1881)

I never realized how exhausting such an experience would be. Surely it must come from being attentive to everyone who speaks up. For some odd reason, I haven't felt anxious. Maybe my resolution about being a silent oyster had something to do with that.

Well, "The Rabbi's Gift" was read. It's one of my old favorite stories, but I never seem to tire of hearing it. It always makes me draw out my internal handkerchief. I thought: "This is such a great story! It's so appropriate in this setting. I'll keep it in mind, it'll be really useful!" Then I promptly forgot about it.

The group was asked to be silent. I had wondered a bit about those silences before I came here. Was I supposed to do anything with that silence? Was I supposed to sit agonizing over how we're doing or was it okay if I went off on one of my internal ramblings? It was a great relief when one of the facilitators said, "This silence is for you." I took it as a sign I could do whatever I wanted with it.

I'm in a very silent sort of group, I think. From the very beginning, there have been long pauses between each time somebody has spoken. I find I like that. I find I like the silences a great deal. So very restful. There was a ticktock from a clock in the background, and it took me back to my childhood summers with my grandmother. The peaceful time when everyone

slept after dinner. More vividly, though, it reminded me of a Quaker meeting I attended in England about a year ago. Then, only one man spoke up during a whole hour.

It sounds boring doesn't it? But the silence in a group is so very different from the silence when one is alone. I think I could easily become addicted to it. Oddly enough, I didn't feel I left the group though I was occupied with my own thoughts. Nor—thankfully—did I feel the need to speak. Others spoke. Many have been so brave from the beginning. I don't know how often I've suppressed an almost overwhelming urge to applaud wildly after someone has opened themselves. How do they do that? Do they get anything out of it? Does it help to be listened to? Some have cried. An old, intellectual part of me says: "This is wishy-washy." But . . . no, I can't help but admire the guts of these people. I'm impressed—especially by the women. They have strength and dignity.

The next session was—interesting. The group is struggling over a very important issue, namely the inclusion or exclusion of a baby. A lovely woman (who gave me permission to write about this) brought along her six-month-old baby boy, Nathan. I noticed it with slight unease, what with babies being apt to make noise at unseemly times and all, but I didn't give it much thought. To be honest, I did my very best to forget there was a baby around. If I didn't see him, maybe there wouldn't be a problem.

Finally someone did acknowledge there was a baby present, and I suddenly realized that the whole group had studiously been ignoring the fact. Might as well have had a twenty-foot troll standing in the corner of the room for all the difference it made. I watched the group start its struggle over Nathan. I had nothing to say—someone else always said it for me.

Yes, indeed, there was a problem having a baby here. Not only was he a child in a group of adults who were there to enjoy adult company, but he would delightedly gurgle his few syllables together at the moment some poor soul was emptying his heart.

Include the child, and it might put others in the group at a disadvantage. Exclude him, and any community the group reaches is a sham.

If I had been forced to make a judgment in the case, I probably would have ruled it a tie and made a cowardly dash for the door before anyone could stop me. Instead I sat it out with the group.

The situation abruptly changed after lunch. The mother had taken matters into her own hands and sacrificed her entire lunch hour to drive the baby home. She returned in a frenzied state. Consequently the group began reminiscing about Nathan, and how quiet it was now. And so on.

Now. From early on, I've been on the lookout for people to dislike. Yes, I know it sounds odd. I'll explain. One of the facilitators mentioned during the briefing how he'd often found that the people he disliked the most in such groups would provide him with the most valuable insights. Not always, but often. That is my general impression as well, and I've wondered whom I would particularly dislike here. During this session, I definitely got a wide choice as I got to know people a little better.

I thought: "You over there, you look like someone I'm slightly annoyed with at home. The way you speak. Your gestures. For Pete's sake stop being that way.

Or, listen to this guy—why does he speak up so often? Does he really feel moved to speak? I mean, I don't feel moved to speak, so how could he possibly be moved so often? Nah he's just compulsively talkative.

Or, I think I'm getting angry with that fellow over there. He's following up people's painful stories with intellectual comments. He's trying to organize things and wrap everything in practical, logical solutions. That's terrible, since that's what I want to do. I want to organize and be logical about people's problems, too. But that's not what they want. They mostly want to be listened to and understood. So I'm sitting here, resisting this enormous temptation to fix people, and you're blatantly trying to fix them. Why can't you be more self-disciplined? Why can't you be more like me?

Apparently, I was not the only one getting my feelings stirred. People started speaking up more often. The silences grew shorter. I felt myself getting a headache, and I couldn't decide whether the tension in the air was due to the thunderstorm outside or that the group was moving into chaos. Or maybe I was the only one feeling tension. I found there wasn't time, suddenly, to digest whatever was said—somebody would lunge in directly afterwards. People forgot to introduce themselves before speaking. Voices were raised. This was rapidly heading into a discussion where everyone wanted to speak at once. It was like watching shipwrecked people in a maelstrom, moving down faster, faster, faster!

A small voice in me grew stronger as this happened. I need silence! It was the closest I'd come all day to feeling moved to speak, so I decided to take the risk of breaking my silent-oyster resolution and finally found a window in the conversation where I could jump in and ask for a couple of minutes of silence. At that point, I thought I would go mad from trying to understand everyone unless I got some precious silence. And just maybe the group would come to its senses. It did calm down afterwards. But that was it. It calmed down, and after the break, it grew even calmer. I thought: I might have made a mistake when I asked for silence.

Several people have thanked me for it, and I've felt thrilled at having behaved decisively—but maybe I was wrong. Maybe I cut the group off in the middle of an important process. And what's happened to the group now? What are we doing? Am I missing something?

For the first time, I look at my watch. There's time left. I had considered my wanting to make the group go through the prescribed stages as quickly as possible. Now it occurred to me that maybe I didn't have to be so concerned about that. I could try to lean back and experience the group as it was. Perhaps this group had its own timing and was where it needed to be. Perhaps.

It occurred to me that I'd found some candidates for disliking today. I knew I disliked them because they'd spoken up and I thought they'd made fools of themselves. Brave fools, but still fools. The next logical step would be to ask what would happen to me if I spoke up at length. People might dislike me! The thought of saying, "Hello, this is the way I honestly am," and being disliked is truly awful.

I was heartily glad when the session finally ended, and I wouldn't have been sorry to see the entire group vanish with a puff. I desperately needed a few moments alone, and the thought of meeting anybody's eye made me shudder.

In the evening it was a different matter entirely. We had circle dancing! Sit me down in a circle of chairs and ask me who I am, and I turn into a mute. Put me in a circle of dancing people, and I can finally show you what's in my blood. Bring in the music, I say! Less talk and more action! Let me use my whole body to express myself, and not just sit there all day moving my head like a drowsy turtle. What's more, I find that dancing is a jolly good way to begin to appreciate those in the group I feel antagonistic toward.

Barrie, Ontario. Friday, July 26, 1996. Second day.

Can't. Won't. Dare not. And probably wouldn't have made it anyway.

(GENTLE TAUNT FROM MIDDLE-NORWAY)

Starting off this morning was a drudge, at least for me. I remembered yesterday's last session and wondered why I'd committed myself to this in the first place—it was getting more boring than interesting. At the same time, I experienced a brief spell of heart-pounding just before the group convened. Apparently yesterday's un-experienced anxiety decided to catch up with me.

The mother had brought Nathan back. I for one was relieved, and the group was decidedly meeker than I remembered it. Whenever Nathan's made any noise today, the group has actually displayed some patience, and the mother has been drifting calmly in and out of the room like a fairy with Nathan in her arms. To my surprise, even I am patient. What's the rush? Children belong in the world as much as adults.

Speaking of patience, I've made an interesting observation. I notice that I have unending patience with the silences and none whatsoever with the people who speak up. Get to the point, get to the point, will you get to the point? Apparently I'm patient enough with situations I've only got myself to worry about, but I have no patience with other people—even when they deserve considerable leeway because they're trying to express deep emotions.

Back to today's first session. The group fell into the usual rhythm of silence—someone speaking up—silence—someone speaking up. The people I was irritated by yesterday behaved

differently today. Either that, or I perceived them differently yesterday. Right from the beginning, people spoke of profound feelings. After a while, I noticed that one of the participants was upset but did not make any attempt to speak. I didn't know what to do. The group shifted into silence and out of silence and nobody seemed to take notice. The group sailed its own painful way, and here was this member all alone being towed along in a lifeboat.

"Should I speak up and invite the participant to open up? Or maybe that is too intrusive. So far, there has been the choice not to speak. Perhaps I should respect that. On the other hand, my heart's pounding and they tell me that's one of the signs that I'm moved to speak. I really feel a need to point out to the group that someone's been crying for ten minutes and no-one has taken any notice of it. If I don't make them aware of that, I think I shall have let the group down. Then again, maybe it's an unwarranted intrusion of privacy."

My dilemma was solved by the participant, thankfully, who chose to speak up. And then I couldn't help but saying afterwards how glad I was for that choice. It's so awful to sit looking at someone who's tortured and not know quite how to be there for them.

Actually, it so happens that I weep a lot during the sessions. When somebody's in pain, I feel inclined to do so regardless of whether or not the person in question does. Frankly that surprises me, because I'm not usually given to emotional displays in public, or even at home. Surprisingly, I'm not embarrassed by it. Nobody's going to point a finger at me for doing so, and nobody seems embarrassed by my displays of emotion. There is one thing that confounds me about weeping for others: My usual way of feeling empathy with others is to see if I've ever experienced anything similar, examine that feeling, and then—maybe—sympathize. Strangely that's not what happens when I'm in the group. I feel others' pain without any intermediate, intellectual stage, and I'm at a loss to explain it. It's as if an invisible barrier I never knew was there has fallen.

All of this is disconcerting. If I show feelings more openly and feel things from the outside more directly, doesn't that mean I'm vulnerable to attack? One blow in this state of mind, and I'll be done for. Now I see what the facilitators mean when they say that community is not only a safe place—it's also a risky place. Since I don't exactly expect to be hurt by anyone, I guess I'll take my chances and string along with the group.

I do know that the part of my defensive system labeled "humor" is laboring under a strain when I'm in the group. Those infernal silences between people speaking rob me of my habit of making clever remarks. I don't know how often I've been forced to bite my tongue these past two days. I never realized how dependent I am on that kind of behavior. If I can make people laugh and myself with them, all is well. If I can't make them laugh, I drag out my store of sarcastic jibes and that'll shut them up. Either way I own the field.

While I'm on the observational track, I've been thinking about power within the group. Yesterday I even toyed with the idea of destroying the group. (Don't be shocked, I did it merely as an intellectual exercise.) This is in contrast to others here who are attuned to the loving aspect of the group—they seem to hear loudly something I only perceive faintly, as through a lot of crackling noise. On the other hand, I have a good nose for power, and I felt sure yesterday that the group's entire power lay in the hands of the facilitators. If I'd wanted to destroy the group's chances of getting anywhere, it seemed clear that only the facilitators could have saved the group.

Today, it's laughable even to have considered destroying the group. I see that they would have been on to me in no time if I'd tried. The power has spread over the entire group and strengthened to the point where you could almost slice it and serve it for dinner. It's more than remarkable.

Speaking of power, I must say it is a little unnerving to listen to people who have lived a lot longer than I have. I hear their tragedies and I get frightened. It's scary being young, and it doesn't get any better from listening to these stories. Will the same things happen to me? It's horrifying to hear the stories of my elders. At the same time, these people are great examples to me. It gives me hope to see that they're still able to enjoy life despite all they've lived through.

Some other things I'm trying to deal with seem to have cultural roots. One is that I can't tell the age of the women around here! It's perplexing. I don't know how many times I've jumped when I've heard a woman speak of sorrows belonging to someone a dozen years older than she looks. I suppose that means these women are actually attaining the magazines' ideal, looking ever younger. Maybe Norwegian women can't be bothered with putting on make-up and eating health food. Or maybe the women here are particularly young at heart.

At any rate, it's embarrassing to find that I haven't been measuring out what I consider the proper amount of respect "for their age." And then that's embarrassing—to find that I discriminate that way. In theory, I would prefer to treat all the souls I meet with equal, unbounded respect, but in practice I tend to fall back on old guidelines.

Another issue with cultural roots is that I can't get used to this openness about emotions. The long, personal stories are all right. The problem comes with the brief statements of joy and hurt, like: "I feel pain when you say that." These just sound

shallow even when I know perfectly well they're not. It's hardest of all to become used to people saying, "I love . . . ." Scandinavians generally express love between mates differently than love between parents and children or between friends. If you say "I love you" to someone, you're pretty keen on bedding down with him or her, and probably for life. So I'm amazed when these people express how glad they are of each other. Apparently, my being accustomed to American television shows hasn't prepared me for this at all. I was so shocked I nearly fell out of my chair when the first "I love you" exploded in the room.

The group sessions really fire my curiosity. I get to hear concentrated bits of other people's lives, and I wonder who these people, these souls, are. What are they like at home, what sort of people are they surrounded by, what do they do in their everyday lives? What's the whole story? Being here is like getting to read a few intensely interesting paragraphs out of thirty or so books. In a day or two, those books will be gone and I'll never know their endings. Or beginnings.

Barrie, Ontario. Saturday, July 27, 1996. Third day.

> *Drawing on my fine command of language, I said nothing.*
>
> —ROBERT BENCHLEY

I made the group a gift today. It'll probably sound eccentric: I normally wear all black when I'm traveling. It's practical, and if you add hat and gloves, even airport staff will treat you with respect. So the group has seen me in rather depressing attire so far, and today I wore some of my favorite clothes from

home. (Even oysters find ways to communicate.) I was glad when people almost fell over each other to tell me how much they prefer to see me in bright green. They were complimenting me, but they were actually complimenting themselves—for making the group such a smashing place to be that I would want to make them the gift of being visually colorful.

I have been getting unwarranted compliments of another kind, too. The fact that I'm the only Norwegian here puts me in a unique position. All of a sudden, I'm seen to carry specialized information just because I come from another country. I could be the village dolt at home for all anyone knows, but here they treat me like a cross between an ambassador and a professor. It's an irresistible position, and instead of feeling humble, I can't help thinking of the freedom it gives me. If I hopped around a house on one leg and told people it was an ancient, Norwegian custom—I'd be believed! I wouldn't, of course, but the possibility is eye-opening. I'm not bound by Norwegian norms while I'm here, nor by American or French or Inner Mongolian cultural traits, for that matter. Nobody can cock an eyebrow at me because they don't know how I'm supposed to behave.

Aside from all that, I must confess that at the moment I'm experiencing a difficult time. My group seems to be such a good place to be in for many. They throw their souls on the table, cry and get accepted. I listen with my heart and try to be there for them, but—?

I heard an insightful question yesterday: "Why don't you let the group be there for you?" That's it. Why don't I? It occurred to me that while I'm in this marvelous place full of opportunities, I behave exactly as I do at home. People generally like to pour their hearts out to me. I'm honored that they should do so, yet it also makes me bone-tired that I'm always the "rock." Many times at work I felt I was not so much selling books as bartending. And now, I'm doing it again! I'm playing bartender to the whole group! When will I ever learn? Listening is the easy way out for me, and I wonder if it's enough.

There are walls within walls, and from what I can see of the next one, it could dwarf the Great Wall of China. Although it's a hindrance to my full participation, I think it's one of those walls that need to be broken down from the inside over a long time. I'm not going to break it down here. I feel I would do violence to my own soul if I were to pull it down prematurely. It makes me wistful to see others plunge in, heart and soul. I dare say I shall be ready myself someday, God willing.

What am I ready to do, then? Yesterday someone took mercy on me and let me pour my heart out for awhile, and it helped. So what do I want from this group? I would like the group to accept me for who I am and I don't think that will be as easy as it sounds. Usually when I'm thrust together with new people, after two or three days the person who's been around me the most will say: "You're so cold!" Ordinarily, I think to myself, "I do act coldly, but if you knew me better, you'd find I'm warm underneath." But what am I to do now that I've shown people parts of my warm side first? My coolness is not just a mask. It's part of my personality. I need it and value it, but how am I ever going to get a group to accept it?

Of course they'll accept me if I tell a sad story and cry. Of course they'll accept me if I show them my wounds and ask for understanding. Of course they'll accept me if I show them some vulnerability. But will they accept my invulnerability? Will they accept the part of me that is crisp and cold like the winter wind? Will they accept me when I tell them I run passionless analyses of them even as I weep for their stories?

Somehow I don't think so. Most people I know don't want to deal with my cold-bloodedness, not even after I've known them for years. My emotional side is fine with them, but my unemotional side is undesirable. They don't realize I feel hurt and angry when they reject this side of me. That's what I fear is going to happen in this group. What will they do when they find out I'm really cold and self-satisfied!

I think a lot about speaking up and getting the agony over with. But every time the group is in session, the subject doesn't seem important anymore. At the same time, I'm watching the group trying to come to terms with another participant who has a passion for being cerebral, and I don't like the proceedings one bit. Then again, if he gets accepted, maybe I can get a free lift.

All this has made me feel like a cornered wolf. I'm increasingly tense as the days move on, and I expect someone to jump up, point a finger at me and cry: "Cold!" any minute now. And it's not going to be meant as a compliment. If this continues, I'm going to feel sick. I know I'm not the only one getting nervous. Several people have become ill and many look harrowed after sleepless nights.

I reached my limit today with "How are you?" The expression frustrates me no end, and "How do you feel?" is even worse. What questions! They seem so out of place. I might not be able to conceal my irritation anymore. If it were one or two people who approached me like that, I would tell them how that feels to me. When there are 130 people bent on asking me how I am, I can't begin to explain my reaction. Besides, they mean well, and for all I know, I may give a lot to hear that question one day.

There is something else I've noticed about people here, and it's their eyes. I noticed before, and more so today, that a kind of softness has come into people's eyes. Soft eyes invari-

ably speak of emotions, and I have a difficult time when people wear their hearts on their sleeves. When I can't turn anywhere without being overwhelmed by another's emotions, it attacks my inner resting place. It feels disrespectful of my preference to retreat emotionally. Also, I'm worried that I might be having soft eyes myself. Anything but that!

Nonetheless, things aren't all so gruesome. We've had some wonderful fresh laughter in the group and, in other parts of the conference, I've actually spoken up in a couple of the special interest groups. What's more, I'm increasingly fascinated by the personalities that are slowly being revealed around me. It's like witnessing the phone booth transformations of Clark Kent into Superman.

I never knew I would see so many good souls in one place. Everyone seems to be bringing a basket full of gifts, and what surprises me more than anything is that even I am able to share from mine. I'm so encouraged by those around me that a bit of divinity pops up now and then before I have time to think twice. What a surprise. I can share, after all.

Barrie, Ontario. Sunday, July 28, 1996. Last day.

Men occasionally stumble over the truth,
but most of them pick themselves up
and hurry off as if nothing had happened.

—Winston Churchill

The Lord's day. Yes, indeed. It certainly wasn't my day. Things didn't look too bad in the beginning. The group had a plunge into chaos, but it was energetic in a good way. On the

sad side, one of the participants left, for reasons of his own, and this created an odd gap. I wonder if the group would have missed me, too, if I'd left.

The bomb sprang some time later. A participant was expressing her joy over the specific presence of a couple of other people in the group. Then she turned to me and told me in a gentle way that she felt I treated her like a rat in a laboratory. I just sat there, stunned. A host of thoughts collided in my head. I've hurt someone without noticing it. I thought everything was okay and now she tells me I've been walking around comparatively happy while she was miserable because of me. How could I fail to see that?

How can it happen that I'm enjoying somebody's company, and then learn later that they didn't enjoy it? Why don't people tell me right away? This is the same old "You're so cold!" all over again. I want to say something! I want to defend myself. But it's five minutes left until the group closes—for good. Five! I'll never have time to say anything sensible in five minutes! I need time to think! Five minutes is not enough.

I'm not really sure of what the group was doing those last five minutes. I remember being outwardly calm—I couldn't have moved if I'd wanted to. I tried to listen, but I was too agitated. The world turned into a series of vague impressions. People speaking. Silences? Standing up. The whole group. To say good-bye. One of the facilitators standing nearby, always so kind. The next clear memory is of sobbing in his arms. I'd hurt somebody and I hadn't noticed it. The group was leaving me now that I finally needed them. I was going to be alone with my soul to try to figure out everything for myself. Again. And then I remembered all the times I've done so before, and cried even harder. Oh, it was good to be held! So good to be comforted. For awhile, the world disappeared.

But time was passing, it was lunch and most of the group had trickled out by now. Those remaining were just waiting to say good-bye to me. So—I gathered my frayed emotions into a tight bundle to say farewell to the gang. I couldn't believe the number of people who had stayed behind to wait for me to come around. That was awfully nice. Then I spoke for some time with the woman who had started it all. I dare say that's something that would not have happened in the "real world."

It wasn't much later in the day when I ran into Doug Shadel, who always manages to look as if he comes directly from a satisfying meal. He offered me a big farewell hug—and I declined. That doesn't sound very nice, does it? What he didn't know was that I'd recently been hugging a lot of people, and I have a love-hate relationship with hugs in general. There's no denying I like bear hugs, and I'd eagerly rushed into every opportunity during the conference. This day, though, I'd had my fill. Strange as it may sound, I was glad I was in a place where I could say "no" to a hug and still be accepted. It was a significant moment for me, because it was the first time I'd deliberately shown anyone my cold side during the whole stay. To my relief, the man was a good sport and seemed to take it with humor.

I first heard about the FCE through Peck's book ***The Different Drum***, and one of the things that impressed me was reading about a fellow crying his heart out—in a group. He made it sound wonderful. I wanted to do that. I figured I had years worth of hardship stored up, and wouldn't it be great if I found a place where I could safely cry for those.

I'd been secretly hoping that something would happen to make me cry in the group, because I don't cry easily, even though I'm able to weep for others. Now that I did get to cry, I feel ambiguous about it. I could have cried more, for one thing; that blasted lunch cut me off when I had about seven years left to sob for. After that, a deadness descended and I couldn't have cried if I'd wanted to.

I did speak with several people over lunch, and they were encouraging and kind. It's like a balm for my soul to know that others can feel this way with me after what happened in the group.

Eventually the conference broke up, and I wasn't too sorry to leave, although it was with an odd empty feeling that I checked into my room in Toronto. Then I jumped sky-high because I didn't recognize the person I saw in the mirror. Judging by the clothes, it was me, but I wouldn't have recognized the face if I had bumped into this person on the street. Was it that my eyes were swollen from crying earlier? Surely a few days of rough-and-tumble community building couldn't have changed me this much . . ..

I went from contemplating this change to trying to recall the precise words that had been said to me in the group. Curiously, I couldn't remember them. The gist of it was that I hurt someone by treating her like a rat in a laboratory, but as to the actual words—forget it! They were gone.

Why was that? The few other blackouts I can point to have occurred in connection with traumatic experiences. It was appalling that I hurt someone, but was the incident traumatic? It took a long time to realize that the reason I felt upset was that I didn't get accepted. My ever-cold, observational side hadn't been accepted, and worse—maybe it doesn't warrant it.

I have been told many times that I hurt people by observing them. How do I deal with that reaction to a part of me I deem valuable? Am I supposed to throw it out? My favorite sentences begin with: "I've been observing . . .." I realize it can be annoying to be scientifically scrutinized, but nobody

seems to remember that I have a heart to balance it out. I need my detachment as much as I need the times I'm close to people. Maybe I wouldn't hurt others if I never spoke about what I observe, but that would be the easy way out for everyone. Besides, I think my ability to observe is a gift. What do I do when others don't like that special part of me?

Trondhjem, Norway. September 18, 1996.

Our prejudices are our mistresses;
reason is at best our wife,
very often heard indeed,
but seldom minded.

—Lord Chesterfield (1694-1773)

I'll tell you what I did. I sobbed all evening and then, just before I fell asleep, I had a curious little vision. I saw my group's facilitators hard at work in a field putting hay up on racks. "What are you putting up?" I asked. "Emotions," they answered. The image was strikingly descriptive. It is well-known in such a wet place as Norway that if you leave hay on the ground to dry, it looks all right until the day you collect it. Then you discover that the whole harvest is destroyed because the bottom side of it hasn't been exposed to air and light. Is that why it's so important to have emotions aired in the group? Do individuals and groups as a whole need to have their dark side exposed to save the harvest?

It's a nice image, and it gave me some comfort when I quietly wept on the bus the next day. It occurred to me that I wasn't at the conference anymore and that people were more likely to be embarrassed by my display of emotion than

to come and put their arm around my shoulder. Still, it hardly mattered.

Before we left the conference we were warned that we were probably in an altered state of consciousness, and I believe I was. I wouldn't normally sit weeping in public places. Nor would I feel so vulnerable as I did those first couple of days after the conference ended. If I ever go to a workshop again, I shall be careful to schedule two or three days afterward where I can be alone to reflect.

It has been a great help to me to be in a community-building group, even if I didn't feel perpetually ecstatic. Groups can behave with civility, and the mere discovery of that was worth the whole trip. I recall feeling like a child again, surrounded by other playing children. Repeated cries of "come on, let's have fun," and a complete lack of self-consciousness. And compliments! I don't know when I've been to a place where people have been so eager to tell each other when they've done something worth applauding. It is encouraging to hear "thank you" for the small things you are and do, and not just the big ones. It teases forth divinity.

Now that I'm back in Norway, I discover I'm more inclined to look for the gifts people have instead of the faults. I've become a little more forgiving of myself, too. And whenever I think I'd better drum up some self-hatred for hurting people, I remember the puzzling moments at the conference when people came up to me and thanked me for something I hadn't realized I'd done for them. It's good to know that even if I unthinkingly hurt people, God sees to it that I unknowingly help now and then, too.

I've even confronted some prejudices I had. People in Europe tend to make what they consider to be harmless jokes about Americans. But nowadays, if I hear any half-mocking

generalizations, I immediately think of "my" Americans who were so brave and compassionate, and I leap to the defense. It's horrible how easy it is to speak without thinking about people's worth. In America, I learned more about honoring other people in five days than I've learned in the last ten years in Europe. I think it's poignant that I should have my soul fished out of the proverbial soup again and again—by Americans.

The more I think back on the people I met, the more I remember their generosity, kindness and courage. The effect seems to snowball. I feel at once humbled and even a bit lost.

Why do I feel lost? I'll leave the question for any sages who might want it. For the same sages, I'll also leave the fact that since I came back, I've dreamed of climbing Hadrian's Wall.

Chapter Eight

Views of Community Building

Since communication is the bedrock of all human relationships, the principles of community have profound application to any situation in which two or more people are gathered together.

—M. Scott Peck, M.D.

BILL THATCHER: I NEVER INTENDED TO BE A FACILITATOR FOR FCE. It was something I backed into. My professional life has been largely made up of working internationally for non-profit organizations. It was as I was embarking on one such assignment in 1987, a workshop in France on team building, that I picked up a copy of *The Different Drum* by M. Scott Peck. I became increasingly excited on the plane as I read the book. Much of what Scott Peck wrote about community building confirmed experiences in my own life.

When I returned to the United States, I wrote to him, and ultimately, I was invited to go through the leader-training program. I made it clear that I was not intending to become an FCE facilitator but they said I was welcome to take part in the training if I thought it would help me in the work I was doing.

Afterward, I thought that maybe I should facilitate at least one workshop, just for the experience. That was ten years and forty-some workshops ago! I have never done anything that was more totally draining than being a community-building workshop facilitator (being a workshop participant is not much easier!). This may be why all facilitators do this work part-time. But I wouldn't trade the experiences I've had for anything. It has helped me in my own work and through difficult times in my personal life.

I have never worked with any group-process model that has been so consistent in outcome. I have facilitated community-building workshops in the United States and other countries, for Fortune 500 companies and non-profit organizations, for public gatherings and private groups. In all of that time and with all of those groups, there has been only one occasion where I can say the group did not come into community to a significant degree. I believe that was because several of the participants attended the workshop in order to evaluate the process for later use. They were busy assessing, comparing and evaluating, rather than participating in what was going on in the room.

The image of a race mentioned in the previous chapter may be helpful in thinking about community building but it is more a marathon than a sprint. It takes endurance training. It often requires every ounce of energy. The concept often described by runners of "hitting the wall" is also an apt description for community building. But whatever image is chosen to portray community building, it needs to include the aspect of training.

Community building is learned. The yearning for community may be within each person but skills are required. That's why I think of community building as a process rather than an event. It is a way of life, not a destination. I can develop the skills I need by following a few guidelines. The guidelines form a way of being toward both myself and others, whether I am in a group or with one other person or by myself.

So what are some of the guidelines?

Acceptance

True community is inclusive; its primary enemy is exclusivity. That doesn't mean everyone in the world must be allowed to be in all groups; the purpose of any group determines how wide the circle is drawn. There are at least two types of exclusivity we have seen in workshop groups. The first is when a group member excludes an individual. The second is when an individual excludes themselves.

Accepting myself can be a helpful starting point. I must start by being willing to include all of me in the workshop process. There are parts of who I am I would rather, even now, keep outside the circle. I can't do that and expect to be fully in community with that group. This does not mean I force any part of myself onto others. What it does mean is that I must not exclude parts of me simply because I don't like those parts. The subject of acceptance has been a lifelong issue for me. Let me share one part of my own story with you.

I believe early on in life I had a strong desire to be accepted by others but didn't know how to get that acceptance. In trying to achieve that elusive acceptance, I made a choice. Looking back on that choice as an adult, I've realized that most of us, as children, try to figure out early on how to get acceptance. Our path of choice to gain acceptance is often a result of one singular experience. Later years are then spent in extended therapy in an effort to find a way to become free of that (usually) ineffective choice. I think it is about as difficult as freeing oneself of an unshielded live electrical cord while standing in water—it can be done but most often requires outside assistance if we are to survive!

My troubles started in the first grade. I was left-handed at a time when left-handedness was not acceptable. The teaching staff at the private Christian school tried to change me—unsuccessfully. But in the process, I got a lot of attention. Attention was a second cousin to acceptance in my mind: not the same thing but in the family. If I couldn't get acceptance, my little boy's mind thought, maybe attention would work just as well! My choice of seeking attention was cemented for me in second grade. I was sitting at my desk with the teacher looking at me, for a reason no longer remembered. I said something and the whole class laughed. I felt the attention. Something "clicked" inside of me and I thought, "Here's how to get what you want!" So began my early years of attention-grabbing behavior.

I became the class clown. I was good at it. My path of attention quickly took me away from the path of acceptance, since teachers saw me as a problem. I added to my skills by also becoming "a smart student who didn't apply himself." Sitting outside the principle's office became a familiar spot for me.

My parents tried many things to get me to change. I enjoyed watching TV. When I was eleven and our TV broke, my parents told me it would not be fixed until I brought up my grades. It was never fixed. I could be winsome and charming at times to those in authority and I think that may have been what kept the school trying to reform me. At the age of sixteen, the school gave up on straightening me out.

The principal held a meeting with my mother and me at the end of ninth grade. He suggested I attend public school, saying that, if I could stay out of trouble, they might admit me for my eleventh grade. I remember driving home with my mother after that meeting. She was crushed. As she cried, she made the prediction that I would never go back to that school. The idea of going to a public school did not seem like a punishment to me at all, but because my mother said I would never go back, I was determined to prove her wrong. I didn't really stay out of trouble in public school but somehow nothing ever got on my record. So one year later, I entered eleventh grade back at the private school.

I was now older and wiser, and I took my behavior "underground." I learned how to skirt the rules without getting caught. That didn't mean I was dull. In the eleventh grade I was elected vice-president, in charge of social events. My class knew I could party. I still didn't study, though. I took Spanish I three times and only passed by promising I would not take Spanish II.

It was during that first year back that I met Pete. Pete was the high school band teacher. I played drums. When offered instrumental options, I determined drums—snare and bass—would be easy. Pete was young, handsome, with a beautiful wife and a great-looking car. As a teacher, he did well with what he had. That's what initially drew me to him. As I got to know him, I discovered he was smart, as well. I found out another thing too. He wasn't fooled by my act. Pete showed me he knew who I was but still accepted me. He befriended me.

So at the age of seventeen, during my junior year, when I thought about becoming a Christian, Pete was the person I went to, to help me decide. It was interesting to me that Pete didn't tell me what to do. He said I already knew what to do. He was right. What he may not have known was that he was the "door" God used to reach me. Acceptance. No conditions.

As a little child, I had wanted—no, craved—acceptance but had only been able to find attention. I didn't want to have to change before acceptance was given. Pete accepted me as I was, with no conditions. Change followed. The type of attention I sought changed. It was because I had encountered, in one person, unconditional acceptance.

Everyone was pleased by the results of my change in behavior but I was still sure that my more acceptable behavior was the condition for their acceptance. My change had been for me, not for them, even though it looked as if I had surrendered. It took a second person in my life to convince me that unconditional acceptance could be a way of life for me.

I met Jan after moving to Seattle. I was several years into my adult life working in Christian organizations and had moved with Anne, my wife, to Seattle for a new ministry. We began attending a Quaker church. I liked the people there, but I found the discussion classes frustrating. After all, I had studied theology in college. I was aware of what was "truth." I judged people based on their theological "correctness," and accepted or dismissed them accordingly.

Jan became the pastor of the church. Her sermons were good and her theology, although slightly divergent from mine, was intriguing to me because she was clearly very bright. So she passed my test.

Jan and Anne hit it off and eventually, along with Jan's husband, Dick, we became a foursome socially. It was on the way back to Seattle, at the end of a weekend spent together on the Oregon coast, that a pivotal event in my life occurred. Jan precipitated it.

We were having a discussion about something that I have long since forgotten when Jan said, "You don't like people do you, Bill?" I was incensed by that comment and responded by saying, "Of course I like people!" Other words were exchanged, but neither of us moved from our positions.

I couldn't believe Jan could think that of me. I was a Christian. Here I was giving my life in Christian ministry for others after majoring in Bible at college. Of course I liked people.

Of course the truth was, I didn't like people. In fact, I even saw people at work more as interruptions to my ministry than as partners. It was embarrassing to me that Jan had seen behind my mask. I was mortified and angry. I promised myself I would make Jan regret her words, and I became cold and distant toward her. The foursome ceased.

The only problem was that Jan didn't respond in kind to me. Her attitude toward me never changed. She didn't force herself on me but she didn't avoid me either. It was so frustrating. I wanted to hurt her and she wouldn't respond. For the second time in my life, I encountered someone who knew who I really was and still accepted me.

As with Pete, so, too, with Jan. I couldn't fit the action of either into my life view. It was a mystery to me. What would make a person accept, even love, me without conditions? When I looked inside myself, it was what I truly wanted but had decided was unattainable—that's why I had chosen attention.

The situation came at a time of crisis in my life. My marriage of ten years was on the brink of collapse and my life of ministry was faring no better. I was not living a life anywhere close to what I had understood I was to be living as a Christian. I was falling apart. I needed help and I needed it immediately.

I went into a period of intensive therapy, culminating in three weeks of isolation therapy in a form somewhat similar to that described in Janov's *Primal Scream.* I remember offering a prayer as I went into my three-week intensive therapy. It wasn't a prayer asking God to save my marriage. It was a prayer asking God to show me how to love the way Pete and Jan had loved me—unconditionally.

It took a week of struggling for me in intensive therapy to accept myself instead of denying who I was and blaming others for who I had become. At the end of that first week I remember the moment I felt freedom for the first time. As I returned to my small beach cottage after the session with my therapist, I was alive to my emotions in a way I could not remember ever being alive to them before. And I actually liked myself. There was plenty of room for improvement but I had some good parts to build on.

The next thing I did was talk to God. It was a simple prayer. Gone was the pride in my theology. I was like a baby. I was starting over. The first thing I did was to admit I didn't even know what it would sound like if God spoke to me. I was afraid I couldn't distinguish between God speaking to me and my own thoughts. This had been the fear that had driven me into the pursuit of theological correctness. I had determined to live my faith intellectually. There was a rather lifeless relationship between me and God. I acknowledged all this in my prayer and asked God to speak to me. He did.

That began a three-day conversation with God that changed my life. I received no unique revelation of knowledge. I simply told God I knew that for me to love the way I had been loved by Pete and Jan would require me to be living in quite a different way than I had been up to this time. I admitted I didn't know how to do it.

An image of a deep hole in the ground came into my mind. God told me that was the entrance to the way of life I was asking to live, and that I had to jump off the edge, into the hole. I argued a bit, and God said, "Well, if you want to live a life of loving unconditionally, this is where it starts." I had been expecting something less scary.

This exchange did at least a couple of things for me. First, it made me realize the seriousness of what I was asking. This was not an easy path. There was danger here! Second, I realized that accepting myself unconditionally was just the first step. I also had to accept God unconditionally. Without that second step, I would spend much of my time requiring God to meet my conditions before I granted acceptance.

Since that time I've realized how fortunate I was to encounter two people who required nothing from me in order to give me their acceptance. It was like a bee finding honey. I also have realized how universal the desire is to be accepted unconditionally. And I didn't have to experience it first before imagining it was possible. The paradox is that I must give it to myself first.

So for me, the issue of acceptance started in first grade. Just because I was left-handed.

The "Rules" Road to Acceptance: My Name Is Marty:

I am forty years old and I was born and raised in Houston, Texas. I went to my first community-building workshop about six years ago. It was a very interesting experience for me. I cried a lot. There were tears and emotions but no words to go with them. I remember at the end of the workshop the facilitators said we were about to end and if any of us had any final comments we wanted to make to the group, we should do it. Now I am someone who is very good at following rules, so I spoke up.

The experience in the workshop I spoke of was a man rescuing a woman in the group. I said to the man, "You know, I would like to say that I have excluded you this entire time because so many times in my life I have wanted a knight in shining armor to rescue me and nobody has. I saw this woman as a damsel in distress and I saw you rescuing her and so I have excluded you." I said this out of anger and resentment that nobody did that for me when I needed it. Saying that to him surfaced for me the whole "damsel in distress" issue, which I had not realized was in me until that workshop.

I have been involved in community building for six years and therapy for five. What I've had to learn is how to take care of myself and I don't want to do that. I resist that. I want to be taken care of, to just have somebody come and rescue me.

My core beliefs are the five principles contained in FCE's Mission Statement: communicate with authenticity, deal with difficult issues, relate with love and respect, welcome and affirm diversity, and bridge differences with integrity. These are with me no matter what. I try to live them every moment of my life. I weigh everything against them.

Listening

Listening is an acquired skill for all except those who are truly blessed! Oh, to have the natural ability of listening that I might, with little effort, hear you. Listening doesn't guarantee understanding but it is essential to the possibility of understanding. Listening is not waiting for someone to finish speaking so I can say what I have to say to them. That's more like two people talking at each other.

Listening is an essential skill for community building. It requires the whole of my body to participate. I listen with my eyes. Distractions more readily come when my eyes are wandering from place to place. My eyes need to supplement my hearing. How do the gestures and facial expressions of the person speaking go with what is being said? The rest of my body needs to be included as well. If I'm jerking around, waving my hands, or walking around when someone is speaking, I distract them and me. Simple? Maybe for you, but not for me. When someone speaks to me, I find I must stop whatever I'm doing and look at them. I hear better when I do, and I let the other person know I'm listening. Listening is an active form of being present for another person.

In community building, listening is a constant activity. I need to listen to others. I need to listen to myself when I speak. And I need to listen in the silence to what may be being said there as well.

My Name Is Karen:

I thought I was perfect. I was going along thinking, "I have had a pretty damn good life, you know? I haven't had all these other problems other people have had and I thought that if they just got on the bandwagon with me, everything would be fine. And then, in the middle of these workshops, I was finally able to start hearing other people's experiences and realized their experiences were not so different from mine. "Maybe I am not quite as perfect as I thought." And the insights just kept coming. I was absolutely locked into an "everything is fine" kind of mentality. I subsequently saw that I am not even close to being fine.

Speaking

A large part of community building involves learning how to communicate. In my first workshop, the guideline given by Scott Peck to "Speak when you are moved to speak and don't speak when you aren't moved to speak," was something I took to heart—that time. I wish I could say I always follow that principle but I don't. The opposite of this guideline—to speak when you are not moved to speak and to fail to speak when you are moved to speak—represents the greatest barriers to effective communication. I've found it sometimes is hard work for me to know the difference.

There are often unexpected emotions that come with speaking when moved to speak. This surprises some people. Why do these emotions come up? One reason I've heard mentioned often is that speaking authentically when moved to speak can open a floodgate of feelings a person has suppressed in order to be accepted by others. The message comes early in life to most of us that there are some things you just don't talk about. Or, if you speak of them, it must be done either unemotionally or in some general way. It feels safer to say, "Divorce is terrible," rather than, "My divorce was terribly painful for me." Sharing who I am with you requires that I speak the particulars of what makes me the person I am.

My Name Is Ardelle:

The first community-building workshop in June, 1995 had more or less of an impact on me. However, I was interested enough to want more, which brought me to the conference in Cincinnati. Don't ask me what happened, but something did. I found myself in a group of mostly men. They were so loving and open. I was amazed by their courage. They were able to tell their dark secrets to a bunch of strangers. I physically started feeling strange: headaches, nausea and pain had me asking myself, "What's my body saying?" No answer came, but on the last morning in the workshop, something inside me pushed and ached to speak. The pain got worse, so I timidly began to speak. "Hi. I'm Ardelle . . .." I had no idea what I was going to say.

I was in awe afterwards. A lot of hate and anger toward men came mumbling out all crooked and with no coherence. It surprised me, given that I am the "peace and love" person, mild and non-aggressive. Where the Hell was that anger coming from? It was a deliverance. I felt fifty-pounds lighter for a week or two. I was in ecstasy. When I got home, I tried to sleep but I couldn't because there was a poem in my head that

wouldn't leave me alone. So I finally gave in and sat down and wrote it. It was a poem for my son. I share the poem so you may understand how the spirit worked in me.

FCE has put me on this path of liberation. It has helped me to accept and love differences and to be more careful of judging others and myself. I thought I was already free of judgment before, but the workshops showed me I still hold some. The love and attentive listening I received in the Cincinnati workshop has greatly helped me to start opening up and getting rid of all the secrets . . . I feel like a flower blossoming into its splendor.

Here is the poem I wrote for my son:

LIBERATION

A young scared innocent woman
Had a sweet son
who she loved very much.
But sadly there was too much
HURT ANGER DESPAIR
in this young, scared woman
To show him all her love.
So the days passed
And all the dear, sweet son could see
was the anger and the despair.
But one day this young woman,
now older and more mature,
was no longer full of anger and despair
Because she had found a way to free herself
For she knew that there was certainly something
Better to fill her life
So now the anger is learning
the despair is learning
the hurt is learning

And she's becoming more and more
full of love
full of hope
full of light
She's freeing herself
She's liberating herself
She's loving herself
to become the beautiful and wonderful woman
she really is
And so the sweet son must also liberate himself
To be able to free himself from the young hurt boy
To become the beautiful magnificent young man
he really is
This is my deepest wish for you, dear Son
Freedom
Love,
Mom

Silence

Many people are uncomfortable with silence in any part of their life and especially so in groups. Most of us have had both good and bad experiences with silence. "A heavy silence filled the room." "He gave her the silent treatment." " Her silent, icy glare transfixed him where he stood." These are just a few of the sentences that can cause cold shivers to run up and down the spine when thinking about silence. We less often think of the "companionable silence between them." The rehabilitation of the concept of silence has only recently begun in our culture.

There is a lot of silence in community building. Some of it can be uncomfortable. All of it can be useful to the community-building process. In *The Different Drum,* Scott Peck says, ". . . silence is the most essential ingredient to emptiness."

My Name Is Julie:

I didn't expect that I would like the silence as much as I did. I got very comfortable with it and came to appreciate it. I was really trying to listen very intensely to others. During the silence, I prayed a lot. I was overwhelmed by the intensity and honesty of people's emotions in the circle.

Integrity

There is a commitment to integrity required in community building. One aspect of that integrity is confidentiality. What is shared in a workshop should stay there. There is no permission given for what is shared by one person to be reported to others by another person. This may be tempting to do but it is one of the quickest ways to destroy community. Participants must show a level of integrity that includes maintaining the confidences given to them by others.

There is another aspect to integrity which can be overlooked: integrity with regard to oneself. Quite often, deep parts of a person's story are shared. But building community is not a matter of just finding the most hidden part of one's being and sharing that part. Community building is not a place to share in an indiscriminate manner. It is rather a place where speaking authentically is most cherished. Speak when moved to speak and share only what you can give yourself permission to share. There are no extra points for the most intimate detail.

My Name Is Karla:

I was a participant in a workshop in Texas. Toward the end of the second day I talked about my father, who had passed away five years prior. I hadn't been present at his death or seen

my father for many years before he died. This was a source of considerable pain for me. With the encouragement of one of the facilitators, I allowed myself to fully experience my grief. I had never given myself permission to feel and express such pain in front of other people before. Nobody said anything until I was done. No one rushed in to offer comfort. The group just held the space for me to be where I was.

Responsibility

Community building does need facilitation. FCE usually has two facilitators for their workshops—one woman and one man. The role of the facilitator is to give the group feedback on the process—not to lead the group. The facilitation process cannot bring a group into community. All it can do is free the participants so the work can take place. When the goal is building community, each participant is responsible for the success of the task. A community is a group of leaders.

My Name Is Andrea:

It was great to cut my teeth on the workshop. I saw my weaknesses—my failure to believe sufficiently in my own gifts and strengths—so now I'm taking many more tasks and being more responsible and active. I am more enthralled with the riches available to me as I speak only when led to speak and conversely the increased self-esteem I have when I speak with full conviction.

Risk

Seldom have I facilitated a community-building workshop where the subject of risk did not come up. It usually is raised in the context of safety. Someone will say, "It doesn't feel safe here for me to take risks."

In my estimation, consideration of risk is very wise. It says, "What I want to share is of value to me and I'm not sure I want to pay the cost I think I will have to pay if I share it with you." Part of the cost of being on the community "road" is this thing we call "risk." Scott Peck has said that risk is the central issue of vulnerability. Without risk, there is no such thing as vulnerability.

My Name Is Michael:

After reading *The Different Drum* I waited for a few years before attending my first workshop. Looking back on it now, I believe I put too much on the group, for I was nearly out of hope. Trusting a group of strangers was easier than being alone with someone in an intimate, vulnerable situation. I hadn't realized how encrusted the shadows in my own soul had become, how sealed off I was from feelings, in or out of my soul. I had not had much interaction with my spouse or children on a heart-to-heart level.

As the group became more real, even though it didn't still feel entirely safe, I had to speak of the difference between what I was and what I was doing and the impact it was having on myself, my wife and my children. This sharing was a different experience, one I had longed for, to speak and not have any comments on it at that time and let what was said filter down into my own soul. Later that day I was able to go deeper, within the safety of the group. Somehow the crust of shadows was broken and light entered my being; there was the touch of a caring hand on my back, tears that once were bitter were now sweet, the hardness broken by love. This was only the beginning of trust in others and myself that there is an unconditional love within each one of us.

Pain

Here's a word that can empty a room fast! There are times when my friends think I'm rather strange because I often talk about the subject of pain. No community-building workshop is complete without this subject coming up for discussion.

In the workshops we are describing here, individuals often share with the group their experiences with pain. In almost all the workshops there is resistance to this. Questions like: "Why do we have to share our pain with one another? Why can't we talk about the good things that have happened to us?" Actually, participants are never told they must share their pain in describing themselves. It just happens. Certainly good experiences are also shared but, time and again, people come back to their pain. "Why do we have to share our pain?" is a good question.

We have legitimate feelings for why we may not want to share pain. Pain is unpleasant. It is also one of the parts of life in which it is easiest to feel most alone. Pain separates us from others. But if we ask, "Why do we have to share our pain?" other questions follow: "Why does pain separate us? Why is loneliness so often a companion to pain?"

A most common reaction for me when someone shares their pain with me is to try to fix them. My motive is to make it better for both them and me! I don't know if that is just a personal response, a male response, or a general human response. The hardest thing for me is to be in the pain with the person and not try to fix it. But I suspect most of us need acknowledgment (being with the pain) more than knowledge (how to make it better) in order to move forward.

Let's take a closer look at failure as it relates to pain. Could this hesitation to share our pain be because pain is associated with imperfection or failure for many of us? There is a prevalent attitude that pain implies some form of failure. The Book of Job, possibly the oldest book of the Jewish and Christian religions, explores the subject of pain and fairness. Friends of Job make it clear that they believe pain is not random. He must have done something wrong. Bad things just don't happen to good people! Job, on the other hand, knows he has done nothing wrong and is even more mystified than his friends.

Pain is not the indicator of failure as we sometimes believe; it is an affirmation that we are alive and still learning. Pain is one of the teachers in the classroom of life.

Let's come back to the earlier question people ask in this community-building model, "Why do I have to share my pain?" There are at least two reasons. First, pain is one of the least acknowledged of all our universal likenesses. It can be a starting point for understanding between us. Pain can bring us together if we choose to allow it. Second, pain is also an expression for each of us of our uniqueness, as we describe our particular experience with it. That is why it is so often shared in the workshops and why facilitators keep encouraging participants to share the particulars of their own story. You will never really know me until you know something of my pain.

Pain is God's megaphone to rouse a deaf world.

—C.S. Lewis

(The Problem of Pain *[Macmillan Publishing, 1962])*

Grace

Grace and trust need to be "word-companions" in community building. Trust is an extremely important quality to possess in community, as well as in life in general. Trust is often thought of as something to be earned. It comes with time and repeated experiences with other people. It can be doled out in ever-increasing measure as others prove worthy. But what happens when trust is betrayed or broken?

I remember a community-building weekend I attended as a participant several years ago. It was a Sunday morning, our final day together, and we were immersed in the issue of trust. Statements of "I don't trust this group . . ." and "It doesn't feel safe here . . ." were being made. As I sat there reflecting on whether I had anything I could offer of myself to the group, I realized that there was one thing I could give. With a voice full of emotion I spoke: "If one of the conditions for being in this group is a guarantee that I can be trusted, I realize I must leave because I'm not always trustworthy. I want to be. I've tried to be trustworthy in the past ,but there have been times when I haven't been." It was the first time I had ever admitted to myself, much less to other people, that I couldn't promise to be completely trustworthy. It was one of the hardest things I was ever able to bring myself to say.

I learned something about myself that day that I've never forgotten: I need grace in community. Grace is un-merited favor extended to someone judged guilty who otherwise would receive deserved justice. It is a way of being toward others, which Webster's dictionary attributes to the nature of God. Grace is a divine attribute. It is something I need from people and something I must also give. It's not something I deserve, otherwise I could just live under the law.

Only I can choose to extend grace to another when I've been wronged, when trust has been betrayed. Grace is not passive. It does not come about by my choosing to ignore an instance of broken trust. Grace is costly action that often flies in the face of both justice and logic.

Grace is different from forgiveness because forgiveness can be given with no offer of future trust. Forgiveness can offer the hope of restoration but grace goes further. Grace restores.

Conclusion

At a meeting of FCE leaders and facilitators in October, 1996, one day was spent considering key aspects of community building. We share some of those comments in Chapter Eleven. Also that day we received a special gift from one of our leaders. As we started the day during which we would be looking at these principles, or values, or words (we weren't quite sure how to term them!), Ellen Stephen read a poem. She had felt moved to write it though it had taken her much of the previous night to complete. What a gift she gave us!

Few, if any of us, who have been a part of FCE have not been touched by the life and witness of E.S. Doug Shadel mentioned in Chapter One her impact on his life. For my part, E.S. has been my traveling companion and co-facilitator through many of my workshops. She has an inner strength that shines with a burning intensity. Here is her poem:

WHO?

The Spirit has no name
except, when pressed by mortal need,
I AM.
She/he/they exist beyond words
(except that beyond, itself, is beyond meaning.)
Nevertheless, in the beginning was the WORD—
the expression of unnameable love
to unimaginable lover,
in the Spirit.
And, but, nevertheless, therefore
the WORD was made flesh.
The cosmic kenotic event,
glory emptied into mortality—

fact of death, truth of life.
The human soulbodyspirit becomes
"the capacity for infinite reality
to be held finitely,"
echoing discretely and uniquely: I am.
This side of the WORD lies autism;
on the far side springs mystery.
And, but, nevertheless, therefore
eternal unnamed love
co-inhabits, co-inheres, communes—
longs infinitely to express
and in deed expresses
I am, you are, we co-exist
and dwell among each other:
glory celebrated,
passion offered,
dailiness received,
in love spoken.

Chapter Nine

Transformation in the Workplace

We trained hard—but it seemed that every time we were beginning to form up teams, we would be re-organized. I was to learn later in life that we tend to meet any new situation by re-organizing, and a wonderful method it can be for creating the illusion of progress, while producing confusion, inefficiency and demoralization.

—Gavis Petronius (A.D. 71)

With almost every adult American spending their time in the workplace these days, swimming in a sea of marketplace logic and conditional love, we wondered whether it was possible for community building to thrive in the workplace.

To answer this question, we decided to survey an organization that has been more involved in using the community-building model with their employees than any other firm in the United States. Over the last three years, 500 employees of Carlisle Motors in Clearwater, Florida, have participated in the community-building model. A 200-question survey was completed by 135 employees (27%) in September, 1996. The findings from the Carlisle study paralleled our earlier general survey findings. The complete Carlisle survey results are listed in Appendix B and some of the data is referenced here in this chapter.

The Carlisle Motors story is an interesting one. When FCE facilitators were first told about the interest expressed by Carlisle in having a community-building workshop, some of them said, "A car dealership? You've got to be kidding!" That seems like one of the last places where the practice of community would even have a chance to get in the door! Then we thought, "Well, this model has been used in a prison and in a nudist colony, so why not?" When we went into Carlisle to interview employees, many of them mentioned how pervasive the culture of "rugged individualism," described in Chapter One, has traditionally been in car dealerships industry-wide. Many of the people we interviewed and surveyed had worked in other car dealerships where the culture was characterized by intense competition, the good-old-boy network, rampant sexism and firmly entrenched hierarchical structures.

One Company's Story

Given this picture of the "typical" car dealership, it is even more amazing that one of the nation's leading dealerships would plunge full sail into the area of community building. Carlisle is a very successful company. They have won the Ford Motor Company's "Chairman" award for customer satisfaction and for meeting financial goals eight of the last eleven years. They are the number one Lincoln-Mercury dealership in the United States and have been for years. In contacting the FCE, they were not an organization in crisis looking for a way to turn their business around. Jim Knowles, human resources director for Carlisle, explains how they became interested:

Our interest in community building started when our senior managers read Scott Peck's *A World Waiting To Be Born.* We

brought in someone to facilitate an internal discussion about the concept of civility described in the book. We got a lot out of that and it created a desire for us to be more open and honest in our communications and to better know and understand each other. We knew a little bit about each other: This guy is married and has two children, this one's divorced and has three children. But beyond that, we really didn't know each other.

So after holding initial discussions, they contacted the Foundation for Community Encouragement and spoke to Robert Reusing. Reusing told them that the best way to learn more about community building was to attend a public conference called a "Community Continuity Conference" (CCC). They then sent four of their top people to Denver in July, 1993, to attend the CCC.

From that experience, they decided as a corporation to take the leap and make community building the ground of their efforts to open communications and build trust and respect among their 600 employees.

In a video tape (described further, below) Scott Wilkerson, president and CEO of Carlisle, described what he hoped community building would do for their workplace:

We measure our employee-satisfaction index through surveys of our associates and while, relatively speaking, as companies go we rank pretty well, there is still, for me anyway, a gnawing sense that we could have a lot more: the trust factor, just among individuals, much less "management versus employees," that sort of thing. I think we have a long way to go there. And speaking from a personal standpoint, there are a lot of personal relationships that have yet to be developed and explored.

Steve Carlisle. executive vice-president and grandson of the founder of Carlisle, had similar hopes about bringing community building to Carlisle:

What I predict is going to happen, is that we are going to go into a room and try to get to know each other a little bit better, and try to cut through the bull and get real with each other and talk about what we are really feeling and say what we think, as opposed to what we think people want to hear.

As we interviewed Carlisle employees in person and surveyed 135 of them, one thing that became immediately clear is that their willingness to risk sharing with each other on a deep, personal level in the workplace setting was a direct result of the commitment and trust modeled by the leaders of the company. As one employee we interviewed, who works in the accounting office, put it: "Its important to know that the top management believes in their hearts that this is the best thing for employees and for the company."

One Carlisle manager, Bill, said the top management's willingness to start the process by going through it themselves and then modeling the process was the key to people accepting the idea:

What was important to me was that people like Jim Knowles and Scott Wilkerson had already gotten involved and they had gone to Denver to check this program out, so they were ready to model it for us. So walking in and having them model it just unbelievably, to me—that's what blew me away, seeing the experience of what happened in that room. I guess it was modeling in the way they opened up and showed themselves as real people, and the fact that they were willing to trust the rest of

us to be exposed to who they are and what they are all about, versus that mask of "I'm the general manager"; you know the role that they play here. And seeing them really for the first time as real people with the same issues that I might have or that anyone might have or that you might hear on the news.

The best way to begin to understand what Carlisle's top management showed the employees is to listen in on one of the very first workshops Carlisle did in 1993. This particular session included owners Wilkerson and Carlisle; Jim Knowles, director of human resources; and several other top managers. (Their comments are taken from the video tape, "Searching For Community, with M. Scott Peck," produced by Trinity Television, the Parish of Trinity Church and the Faith & Values Channel, of New York City, and the Foundation for Community Encouragement and the National Interfaith Cable Coalition.)

As you read these comments, think about how these very successful men are struggling with the culture of rugged individualism and the balance between their personal lives and their professional lives. Also, try to envision whether or not you could see the CEO and top managers of your firm speaking together in public on such a profound level.

My name is Brian:

Steve, you were explaining or defining your role in the company and in doing so, what I had heard was that you were almost asking for approval. You felt that you were spending more time with your children and with your wife and you have less responsibility for the day-to-day activities and it almost sounded like you were asking for us to say that's okay. I guess that's been going through my mind ever since you said that.

Because it seems so odd to me . . . being that you are a principle of the company, it would appear to me that it would be your right.

My name is Steve:

I think that one of the reasons I was asking for that permission or just letting people know, if you don't see me around that may be where I am. It's been a competitive place. Carlisle Motors is made up of a lot of high-performance people and I guess I am a competitive person, too. I guess I always feel the responsibility to carry my own weight. I don't want to just be somebody that just sits there and makes the money from everybody's labors. I feel a responsibility to earn my keep, too. And I am insecure about it a lot and I have had a lot of paranoid feelings, being the third generation in this business, that I have been handed everything on a silver spoon and that I am not worthy of it, or whatever.

I am conscious of all the feelings of how many businesses don't make it into the third or fourth generation because—you know, my father is a very high-performance person and a very special person himself and its very hard to live up to that standard that my father and grandfather have set. It puts a lot of pressure on you, and sometimes it gets to you and you start feeling like you're not worthy to be in the position that you are in. I have tried this summer, since my kids have been out of school, to work on my family relationships, and spend time with my son or my daughter.

My son Jeffrey is eight years old and he is just absolutely hungry for my attention and it's cool, because I can give it to him. He and I have a lot in common and we're becoming bud-

dies and that feels really good. But I am conscious of the fact that maybe I'll take my kids to swim practice and come in late, or some days I don't come in at all or some days I come in dressed casually instead of in a suit.

With my perception of the environment at work, I see this standard up there of what Carlisle people are supposed to be and supposed to look like and supposed to act like and I know a lot of you and the people back at work are putting in, you know, 80-hour weeks, it seems like. And I, being one of the owners, probably profit more than anybody else and it creates guilt, you know?

Is this money that I earned or did I just happen to be in the right place at the right time? Anyway, it feels good to talk about it and get it out, then maybe I can get on with something more important.

My Name is Jim:

What you've just said, Steve, is what in my estimation "community" is all about: developing relationships. And you have seized the opportunity and I think that it is just growing out of our community building here. You are seizing the opportunity to develop relationships with your kids. And I think we all yearn to do that. Deep down within me, I keep saying it. I am a provider, but I keep saying to myself, "What price am I willing to pay to develop a real bond with my kids?" I think that you are moving out to bond with them. I still don't know what price I am willing to pay to really bond with them. I keep bringing it up. And I don't think that I have paid the dues, if I can use those words, to develop the relationships that I really would like to have with my kids.

My Name is Dick:

And I would say to you, Steve, that's good what you are doing because I have four grown children and I don't have a relationship with any of them. My father was a provider and I was a provider and I didn't build a relationship with them. I have always been a work-aholic and I guess I have chosen that as my profession. I have spent 50, 60, 80 hours a week at work since I was 20 or 21 years old and never developed a relationship with my children. So I think its really neat that you are doing that.

My name is Joe:

Dick said something that struck a heavy cord in my heart and it related to what Steve had said earlier about his feeling of guilt. And when Dick made a comment about—I've heard him say it before—about the relationship with the children, it never really hit home until hearing it along with what Steve said about the guilt feeling. I have always had a lot of guilt because—this might sound crazy—I have a wonderful relationship with my three sons. One's graduating from college, the other two are in college, they are great at everything they do, they are good kids. But I have always felt guilty that I have put so much time into them, that the career that everyone always expected—that where I am at my age—I have always felt like a failure there. But after hearing what . . . it's difficult . . . I guess I'm not a failure.

The willingness of these top managers and leaders of Carlisle to open themselves up in front of each other has been enormously important to getting the rest of the organization to participate. After the initial community building workshop with top managers, Carlisle embarked on an ambitious schedule of community building workshops at all levels of the company, with top managers participating in many instances right along side auto mechanics, service managers and bookkeepers.

One such bookkeeper, Melissa, has seen the improvement in the culture of the organization, especially as it compares to other car dealerships she had worked at in the past:

I want to say that I have worked in a number of car dealerships before coming here to Carlisle. They were all the same and Carlisle is by far the exception. Here is what it's like in the other dealerships: If you didn't wear a tie, you had no brain; if you were a woman, you were totally clueless—you were a blonde bimbo whether you were blonde or not, you knew nothing. It was extremely sexist, with power struggles, severe turf battles, no openness, no honesty, a lot of hidden agendas; what upper management was doing was a secret. If somebody was let go, it was a secret, you couldn't say, "Excuse me, what happened?"

Here, we had a situation several months ago where a salesman was let go. He was one of our favorite salesmen, and we went to the sales manager and asked what happened, because we couldn't possibly understand why this person would be let go. Very honestly, very directly, they told us what happened and said, "It was unfortunate, but it happened." And I had never, ever, worked at a place where that kind of thing is possible, where you feel like you can go to them and say, "Help me understand this," and they will honestly help you.

Bill agrees about the difference between the corporate culture at Carlisle and that of other dealerships:

I have worked in other car dealerships in the past and it is terrible. They are controlling, giving people in positions of

authority all the power, talking down to people—the way they treat people by firing them just 'cause they're mad at them and replace them with another body. I have seen people come and go in this company who have been excellent at what they do but community building forced them to leave. A lot of people have left. And when I think about those people, how they were brought up is the reason they are the way they are, and it's also the reason they are successful at what they do business-wise and profit-wise.

The culture here is different from all the things I learned growing up about working for managers and supervisors: the whole Machiavellian approach, back-stabbing, doing whatever it took to get ahead in the business world. And whatever roles these people are playing out there to get what they want to be successful, this is what it has taken to be successful in my experience in the past. I have watched people go through all those steps and do all that stuff. If other businesses want that kind of culture to exist in their company, then stick with the way it's been and don't do community building. But if you want to treat each other with respect and dignity and be open and honest with each other and still turn a profit, community building can get you started along that road.

In our survey of Carlisle employees, we asked a series of questions about how community building had impacted the workplace. We said:

> **Please indicate how well each of the following descriptions reflects the atmosphere of your particular workplace environment immediately before the community building workshop and now.**

WORKPLACE

(Percent answering "Very" or "Fairly")

	Before	Now	% of Change
Workplace has a high degree of teamwork	65%	86%	32.31%
Workplace has a lot of turf battles	61%	43%	-29.51%
Easy to communicate openly and honestly with co-workers	57%	88%	54.39%

These dramatic improvements in the areas of teamwork, reduced turf battles and open and honest communication have been achieved by a combination of community building and an aggressive on-going program of teaching and refining individual's communication skills through weekly training sessions.

The effect of this community building on employees has been dramatic and it has created intense loyalty by employees. Melissa makes no secret of her loyalty to the firm:

The practical effect of this type of management approach is that I know I can go to any dealership in this county and make a hell of a lot more money than I am making right here, but it ain't gonna happen. I have had several job offers from different dealerships, but I like working here so much that I don't even consider moving. And it is also because 95% of car dealerships are the same as I described earlier. I know when I was working at another dealership, there were people who moved to other dealerships thinking the culture would be better, only to find that it was the same. It's an old-boy mentality.

Jim Knowles, in his role as human resources director, has noticed numerous ways in which improved communication has helped their business:

There are lots of examples of how community-building principles have helped us, but primarily it comes down to improving communication: people used to not communicate with one another, and therefore not address the issues that need to be addressed to make us more productive.

Miscommunication is the single biggest problem we have and that is why we are spending so much time and money trying to communicate better. If we can learn to communicate better, then there will be less misunderstanding, because we are taking the time to hear. Let me give you an example.

We had a technician who was on the Blue Team who wanted to be transferred. In the old days, we would have transferred him. But the director of fixed operations brought him in to his office, along with his supervisor, and said, "Why do you want to be transferred?" The technician said, "I don't know, I just want to be transferred." Well, it took awhile, maybe thirty or forty minutes, but we finally got to the reason for the transfer request.

Three months before, the supervisor had said something to the technician that had left an impression that the supervisor didn't respect his technical talent, and that therefore he wasn't going to be given the tough jobs. This was eating at the technician but he never brought it up until his stomach was churning all the time, and he finally asked for a transfer.

But they worked it out; the supervisor heard the explanation, and the technician felt respected and no longer wanted to be transferred from that team. They had opened the lines of communication.

We probed the issue of communication in our survey in two separate areas. First we explored the barriers to authentic connection with others by asking:

> **Rate the following in terms of the barrier it presented to you personally connecting with others immediately before the community-building workshop and now.**

Here are selected findings from the 135 individuals from Carlisle who responded to our survey:

SIGNIFICANT BARRIERS TO CONNECTING

(Percent answering "Very" or "Fairly")

	Before	Now	% of Change
Hard to find people to trust	65%	32%	-50.77%
Unable to lower my defenses (social mask)	46%	15%	-67.39%
Fear of being judged	41%	13%	-68.29%
Feeling misunderstood	37%	11%	-70.27%
Fear of rejection	36%	14%	-61.11%
Fear of weakness	20%	12%	-40.00%

You will notice from these data that the single largest change occurred in the category "feeling misunderstood," which seems to be validated by Jim Knowles's example of the misunderstood mechanic.

Because there was such dramatic change in the reduction of barriers to connecting with others, we also wanted to know whether individual employees felt more connected to each other and to friends and family as a result of the community-building experience. In our survey, we asked:

How would you rate your feeling of connectedness to the following people before the community-building workshop and now?

FEEL CONNECTED

(Percent answering "Very" or "Fairly")

	Before	Now	% of Change
Yourself	89%	98%	10.11%
Co-Workers	79%	94%	18.99%
Boss	63%	81%	28.57%
Acquaintances	57%	77%	35.09%
Neighbor	52%	72%	38.46%
Stranger	21%	48%	128.00%

Some found the workshop to be extremely helpful in improving interpersonal relationships and connectedness in people's work life. For example, Bill:

I've worked here 15 years and I have worked with people that whole time and didn't really know them—didn't have a clue about their personal life. Didn't have a clue. And it dramatically changes the way we interact with one another. A good example of that is Scott Wilkerson, the president of the company. I

mean, I always thought he was an okay guy—I had had one or two dealings with him where he was in his role as president of the company, doing his job. But if I walked up to him then, before community building, and had a conversation with him, it was completely superficial— "How ya doing, see ya later"—and I don't want to spend any time around you 'cause you are who you are." I was intimidated by that type of thing.

And afterward, its a whole different feeling. Now I can walk up to him and have a personal conversation and none of that other stuff exists. He's not the general; its just him and me, as human beings, talking about whatever. Business can come into it, and then he is the general and we can revert to those roles. But community building made me realize that they are just roles, nothing more and nothing less.

I have begun to see people as human beings first and business colleagues second and that has made a big difference. And this is true for every single person who was in that room doing community building—that shift happened over the three days. Now they are real people.

Bill and many others at Carlisle are quick to say that the community-building workshop provided a foundation of trust and respect upon which to build closer relationships with each other, but that maintaining that closeness was difficult and required additional work and training. Says Bill:

The workshop impacted the way I dealt with people very intensely right afterward. You know, you go to a community-building workshop and you are kind of high on it for awhile—two, three weeks, or whatever. I can remember after one workshop, I came home Sunday night and Monday morning I remember going out to my car to go to work. It was still dark outside and I

stepped outside of the garage with the door open, just staring at the sky for, like, ten minutes, you know? And my wife looked out the door and said, "What are you doing?" My mind was going a hundred miles an hour—it was almost a numbing for me because I had so many personal revelations during the workshop.

But unfortunately, after a short while, that high kind of goes away. It is very easy to fall back into the normal patterns of interacting with each other: the sarcasm, the jokes. That's why the on-going communications classes have been so important. Community building got us started and built a foundation of trust and now the communications classes we have been taking have helped us in carrying it along.

Bill's view of the role of community building as a foundation upon which future learning could be built was shared by almost every employee we interviewed. FCE and its facilitators have long known that organizations that look at a workshop as only an event will never derive full benefit from the experience. Just as it is for individuals outside the workplace, community building is "a way of being together" for people in workplace settings. It requires discipline and commitment for change to be sustained over the long haul. Carlisle has been consistently willing to remain committed to having community building saturate their structure as our research data has shown.

With regard to the on-going communications classes to which Bill alluded, since October, 1995, Carlisle has had their ten senior managers meeting in a facilitated session every Friday for four hours, just to learn how to communicate more effectively. But they haven't stopped there. Said Knowles:

We have one hundred other formal and informal leaders who are going through a similar process. They are in five dif-

ferent groups of twenty and have been meeting since January, 1996 for two hours per week, learning the same things: learning how to communicate, learning how to become better listeners, basically using the same process.

In July, 1996, we started a similar thing with the rest of our employees. We are giving them a six-week session so that everyone in the company has the opportunity to see what the leaders are going through. We want them to understand our interpersonal communications goals as a company. There are eight primary objectives:

1. To become more aware of myself and my feelings in the here and now—to begin to share that experience with others.
2. To learn that my own perceptions and feelings are my own—not necessarily the truth.
3. To learn to increase my awareness of my own feelings and to differentiate them from my thoughts, beliefs, judgments and values.
4. To learn to express more clearly and directly without intellectualizing, generalizing, or using "you" statements.
5. To accurately hear what others say and to monitor my own reaction of that experience.
6. To concentrate on my own growth rather than on others.
7. To become aware of my own "issues" and defense mechanisms: rationalizing, minimizing, discounting, attacking, blaming, placating, distracting, and the impact of those on others.
8. To learn to appreciate what is alike and different about us and to gain a genuine acceptance of them.

This ambitious agenda of improved communication and really sophisticated understanding of human psychology appears to be paying off at Carlisle. We said:

Rate the following in terms of its importance to you immediately before the community-building workshop and now?

THE IMPORTANCE OF—

(Percent answering "Very" or "Fairly")

	Before	Now	% of Change
What others think of you	73%	58%	-20.55%
Accepting yourself for who you are	71%	95%	33.80%
Accepting others for who they are	69%	88%	27.54%
Living authentically	66%	91%	37.88%
Finding meaning in your life	62%	88%	41.94%
Learning about the experiences of others	53%	81%	52.83%
Material possessions	52%	42%	-23.81%

Scott Wilkerson, president and CEO of Carlisle, saw changes in the corporate environment within six months after putting people through the process, but he is realistic about the long-term challenge of maintaining community:

Six months after over a third of the company participated in the workshops, there is no question that the withholding, the distrust, has diminished greatly, especially among the workshop participants. We have a long way to go as a compa-

ny. It's a day-to-day continuous effort, because whenever problems arise, that's really where the rubber meets the road, as far as I am concerned. Are we willing to empty ourselves of our ego, empty ourselves of whatever. Are we willing to address this conflict in a manner that we are used to or are we going to try to do it from a place of community.

Yesterday, I came out of a community-building session that was absolutely wonderful, with about 26 other people. And then I came back to work and there were two departments fighting with one another, on something that had been simmering and brewing and it had broken down into a total lack of communication; all the communication had been happening through rumors and asides and presumptions—just like the good old days

So I took a deep breath and thought, okay, how do we want to address this? And I didn't make a decision for them, which is what they wanted me to do. I just talked about the principles of community and sort of reminded them and said, "Well, let's try this again."

I think we have to remind each other every day, especially when there is conflict. Its easy to be in community when there are no problems, when we're in the circle and everything is beautiful, but come back to the everyday realities of egos and pay and an hour's work and power and authority. We have to remind each other.

One of the things that Carlisle management worries about from time to time is the potential disruptive effect community building can have on the families of its employees. The profound psychological changes which our surveys have documented clearly must have an impact on those family members who do not work for the company. We heard from a Carlisle employee in Chapter Six who described the ways people around her have noticed that she has become more open and accepting and less judgmental as a result of going through both community-building and communications classes. She told how she says "I love you" now to her father, whereas for 33 years, such a thing was unimaginable.

We furthermore have seen consistently that participants report a dropping of the social mask and stronger sense of connectedness to various other people in their lives. But not everyone has been able to embody the principles and discipline of community without experiencing turmoil and suffering. Bill is an example of someone who was "blown away" by his community-building experience and has grown tremendously as a result. But it did create complications in his family life:

One of the insights for me had to do with my marriage. Community building made me so aware of what I needed and how unhappy I was playing the role I was playing, that it forced me to make a move. After the workshop, my thoughts were churning and as I continued to go to workshops, the insights kept coming. It was a lot about myself and who I am, versus the role I was playing as a husband and father. Did I make the right decisions along the path? It turns out that my biggest insight was that I had made some wrong moves and I needed to make it right.

As I became more and more aware of myself and my own feelings, the result was that three years later I was divorced and now I'm trying my best to be a great father. My wife told my son at one point, "Your father is not modeling what it is like to be in a family—you can't run away from your problems." I said to him, "Well, sometimes it takes more strength to stand up to what's going on than to just go along with it."

And so my biggest struggle now is in my relationship with my son—I have an eight-year-old son and my struggle is to discover how can I be divorced and still be a great father to my son—is that possible?

So Bill openly acknowledges that the insights he gained from the workshop caused him to re-evaluate his life situation, and, ultimately, he decided to move on. But despite the pain and anxiety such a life-changing decision has caused him, he reflects now on how it was clearly something he needed to do and that for him it was the right move:

Despite my struggles, the most profound insight I have gotten from my experience with community building is that I now have the courage and the freedom to be myself.The hardest thing that I have done is to own up to who I am. I have the freedom in my personal life because I created it, but this company is allowing me the freedom to be myself and run my department and that's the biggest impact for me here. Because, in the role of husband, I was also playing the department role, which had certain restrictions and do's and don'ts and "carry yourself a certain way." Now I feel much freer both personally and professionally to just be myself. I have learned that being myself is good enough. I accept myself.

Conclusion

Carlisle Motors, more than any business in the United States with which we are familiar, has embraced the principles of community building. Not only have they invested a significant amount of time and money in teaching communication skills to employees, but it has also changed the way they do business. Beginning in June, 1996, Carlisle went to a one-price, no-negotiating system of selling cars. Jim Knowles says that the values of authenticity and openness they have gotten from community building caused the change:

In our previous system, if you were a tough negotiator, you could get a better deal on the identical car that someone else who was not a strong negotiator paid. We concluded that this was an inauthentic way for us to do business. And furthermore, it forced our employees to be one way at work and then go home and be a different person there. There was no congruency.

Knowles says that Carlisle looked at going to a one-price system back in 1992 but focus-group research showed that their customers didn't want it, so they abandoned the idea. Community building has compelled them to do it anyway, the research notwithstanding:

Now our commitment to the values of community building—our desire to bring together the way we want to live in our personal lives with the way we are in business—overrode the research from focus groups.

The result of this move was to experience a massive exodus of top salesmen who felt that the one-price system would reduce their profitability. It is not clear at this time how the one-price system will change Carlisle's profitability. What is clear is that during the preceding three years, while over 84% of their work force was participating in community building, their profits were higher than ever. During the period of 1993 to 1995, Carlisle's operating profits soared by more than 47%. In addition, their customer satisfaction scores, which Ford gives them, based upon customer surveys filled out by each consumer who buys a car from them, have been the highest they have ever been in the long history of this very successful company.

The corporate philosophy of Carlisle reflects the community-building principles and, in case we had any question about how seriously this firm takes their new philosophy, as we were leaving Carlisle Motors, Jim Knowles gave us a laminated card that they distribute to all employees, which carries their corporate philosophy. The card reads:

Long-term profitability through customer satisfaction.
Customer satisfaction through employee satisfaction.

PRINCIPLES FROM COMMUNITY-BUILDING EXPERIENCE:

- ▲ *Relate with Love and Respect*
- ▲ *Communicate with Authenticity*
- ▲ *Deal with Difficult Issues*
- ▲ *Bridge Differences with Integrity*
- ▲ *Celebrate Individual Differences*

In our work to empower others, we remember our reliance upon a Spirit within and beyond ourselves.

One of the key insights we have gained from studying the Carlisle example is this:

> Organizational communication is a function of the individual employee's ability to communicate.

So often, business leaders will look at their operations and the systems and structures in place and make adjustments as though the moving parts (people) were pieces of sheet metal.

Transformation in the workplace must occur at the level of the individual employee if one is ever going to improve the overall system. Carlisle started helping employees learn about themselves and each other at a personal level (community building) and, once trust and respect was established, they moved on to helping individuals learn and practice communications skills (the six-week communications course), which minimized misunderstanding, streamlined organizational communications and ultimately led to improved profitability.

Finally, once they had spent a prolonged period of time working at the level of the individuals in the organization, the system-wide structures they had in place for over a generation were deemed to be obsolete and they transformed the whole system by moving to a one-price, fair and simple pricing structure.

This process is not easy and no business should undertake it unless they are willing to go the distance, as Carlisle has done. But those that choose to do so will likely find that the employee productivity is enhanced, communication is streamlined, turf battles are minimized and teamwork and cooperation flourish. These things, taken together, can only lead to one thing: PROFIT.

Recommended Reading:

Peck, Scott. 1993. *A World Waiting to Be Born.* New York: Bantam Books.

Senge, Peter. 1991. *The Fifth Discipline: The Art and Practice of the Learning Organization.* New York: Doubleday.

Senge, Peter, et al. 1994. *The Fifth Discipline Fieldbook: Strategies and Tools For Building a Learning Organization.* New York: Doubleday.

Section Four

The Principles and Practice of Acceptance

Chapter Ten

The Call to Authenticity

In the world to come, they will not ask,
"Why were you not Moses?"
They will ask,
"Why were you not Zusya?"

—*Zusya of Hanipoli*

ONE OF THE MAIN SUB-THEMES THAT RUNS THROUGH THIS BOOK is the idea that we are called to be authentically who we are, as opposed to who others may want us to be. The tension between living as our essential authentic selves versus the existential social self others want us to be is, we have argued, one of the fundamental struggles of human existence.

But following one's call can be the single most difficult thing one can strive to do in this conditional-love world of ours. How many of us are truly following our call? Would we even know our call if we saw it? In *An Open Life,* Joseph Campbell, quoting from Fredrick Nietzche's introduction to *Thus Spoke Zarathustra,* describes the three stages of the human spirit and it is a powerful description of the struggle we have when we seek our true purpose:

> The first stage is the camel. The camel gets down on his knees and says, "Put a load on me." This is the condition of youth and learning. When the camel is well-loaded, he gets to his feet and runs out into the desert. This is the place where he is going to be alone to find himself and he is transformed into a lion. And the function of the lion is to kill a dragon and that dragon's name is "Thou shalt." On every scale of the dragon, there are the words "Thou shalt," which represent the rules and obligations of society. But the lion is strong and he kills the dragon and is thus transformed into a child. The child is then like "a wheel rolling out of its own center." The way to get in touch with that child rolling out of its own center is to respect the rules of society but to nevertheless go your own way.

Part of the trick to becoming a "wheel rolling out of its own center" is to follow and practice the principles of acceptance. For only by accepting ourselves unconditionally and remembering that we are unconditionally accepted by a loving God, can we begin to muster the courage to live what we are authentically, perhaps even divinely, called to do. Nietzche's description also suggests that the goal is to become increasingly inner-directed, depending less and less on the opinions of others for direction.

But this is all easier said than done. People clearly yearn for acceptance, but most often the still and small voice directing one's call is drowned out by the roar of the culture. Quieting that roar and discerning one's call is an essential part of what it means to be human.

Simply put, the universe does not make spare parts and each and every one of us has something we can do better than anyone else. And it may not be what our father or our mother or our favorite professor or our minister wanted us to do. It may not be that which makes us the most money or which gives us the most television exposure or the most adulation from an adoring public or the most power to wield public resources. The call might be as simple as being a gardener or a receptionist or a welder or a painter. Only you in consultation with your higher power can discern your calling. The only thing about which we feel certain is that everyone has one.

The call is to authentically live one's life until one is complete. There is a discussion in Chapter Four about the Greek word teleios, which, while technically defined as "to be complete," appears in many translations of the New Testament as the word perfect. Some then interpret this as support for the idea that we must strive for perfection in everything we do. Our belief is that we should strive for "completion," not perfection. And what it means to be complete for you will undoubtedly be different for the next person.

The research we have conducted, surveying the impact on people of community-building workshops, indicates consistently that people feel freer to live authentically once they have experienced the healing power of acceptance by a group. Here are some of the findings from both the general survey of workshop participants and the Carlisle Motors's employees' survey, on the subject of authenticity:

AUTHENTICITY

(% answering "Very" or "Fairly")

	Before	Now	% of Change
IMPORTANCE OF LIVING AUTHENTICALLY:			
General Survey	94%	100%	6.3%
Carlisle	66%	91%	37.9%

ACCEPTING YOURSELF FOR WHO YOU ARE:			
General Survey	87%	100%	14.9%
Carlisle	71%	95%	33.8%
IMPORTANCE OF WHAT OTHERS THINK OF YOU:			
General Survey	81%	48%	-40.7%
Carlisle	73%	58%	-20.5%
CONGRUENCE (BETWEEN AUTHENTIC AND SOCIAL SELF):			
General Survey	61.0%	93.3%	52.9%
Carlisle	59.9%	77.9%	33.3%
COMFORTABLE REMOVING MASK:			
General Survey	57.3%	82.1%	43.3%
Carlisle	54.1%	84.8%	50.3%

We learned of an interesting individual who clearly lived his life authentically despite the consternation or disapproval of other people.

In July, 1996, a man named Rusty Meyers gave the keynote address at the Foundation for Community Encouragement's Ninth Annual Community Continuity Conference in Toronto. A long-time facilitator for FCE workshops, Rusty was asked to address the subject that was the theme of the conference: emptiness. From a spiritual perspective, all of the great traditions have described the practice of emptying or non-attachment or meditation as the doorway to closer connection to creation or God. It can also be the doorway to acceptance. Emptiness is the third stage in the community-building process.

Although the FCE model of community building does not espouse a particular religious perspective or even mention the word *God* anywhere in its literature, as a matter of practice, there is clearly a spiritual dimension to the process. As one participant told us when we asked why she reported that she felt closer to God during the workshop, she said, "When you strip away all of the noise and busy-ness of the our day-to-day existence, what is left?"

There is a link between being able to empty oneself of the existential noise of our world and mustering the courage to identify and follow one's call. It could be that one is a precondition of the other. Only by quieting down and listening to the still small voice inside can one even begin to understand one's authentic purpose.

Rusty spoke of a number of things during his keynote address to some 150 FCE facilitators, participants and leaders that July day in Toronto. It was a deeply moving presentation, too lengthy to include here in its entirety. But there was one story he told that illustrates the point about having the courage to follow one's call. Rusty described a man he had known throughout his life named Ray. Here is Rusty's account of Ray and of their relationship:

Ray was right there when I was born, according to him. I just remember him from my church, when I was a little boy. Part of my growing up was to be at the Presbyterian church every Sunday from seven in the morning until one in the afternoon, and Ray was the custodian there. I was told by an older person that he was actually at one time the most popular professor at a major university in the Midwest. Apparently, prior to World War II, Ray was the primary draw to the university, where he taught anthropology, comparative religion and phi-

losophy. Sometime right after the war, he just walked away from it and no one quite knew why.

So there he was, the custodian at our church. I was always aware as a kid that he was around and that he was significant to me, but I don't remember any transactions or even talking to him. All I do remember is sneaking into his little hideaway—it was a closet that was hidden away, down in the basement of the church—where he evidently read: he had a lamp and a mattress on the floor. I would just sneak in there without letting him know, thinking, "Well, I am going to get something by standing in this closet."

Later in my life, I went back to my hometown and worked as a banker. I was a runner, too, and when I got up at sunrise and ran through the streets, Ray was always up, too, riding his bicycle. And that is when I got curious about him. I found out that he watched the sun rise every morning through the huge window of the Presbyterian church. At the end of the day, he would watch the sun set through the huge window at the Catholic church. And each day he made his rounds, visiting people at housing units for the elderly and at hospitals.

I was a hospital board member and once when I came out of a board meeting, I saw him in the hall, and so I followed him. A nun noticed me following him, and spoke with Ray. I couldn't quite make out what they were saying. And then the nun said to me, "Well, you would never figure it out, but he helps people go where they need to go when they need to die." I thought about that a little bit and then she looked me in the eye and said, "He's a healer."

After a while, Ray was fired from his job at the church because many times when I would come to church—in the 1950s in the Presbyterian church, you would always be dressed up, even me as a little kid, I would wear a bow tie and a little sports jacket—Ray would be in his shorts with no shirt on in the summertime, taking care of the gardens. Sometimes he would listen to the sermon, I think. But just before the anthem was going to be sung, he would slip into the back of the choir loft and sing the anthem. We always wore robes, and so he'd throw a robe on over his bare skin and his shorts.

He went to the beat of a different drum, what else can I say? The weather and the sun and the conditions of something else greater than the cultural norm was what was directing Ray.

After he was fired, he became the towel person at the YMCA. And the kids loved him, including me. He never said anything profound or special. He just smiled and paid attention to you. You felt like you were important when he gave you a towel. He was serving you. When he took a shower, he'd be in his birthday suit doing yoga while showering, so they fired him for that; they didn't think that was appropriate. And I don't really recall whether he got another job or whether he worked after that or not. You know, he was getting older. I was in high school, went away to college and then taught in another city and so it was several years later when I moved back to my home town and became aware of him again.

One of things in the business community in that town, a town of about 52,000 people, was that there were "Ray" jokes. If you went to any kind of gathering of business people, somewhere sooner or later in the course of conversation, or in trying to figure out the pseudo-conversation taking place, people would tell jokes, including ethnic ones, and there also would be a "Ray joke." Ethnic jokes always made me uncomfortable, but "Ray jokes" made me particularly uncomfortable.

There were always kids around Ray. I mean, when we were at the municipal swimming pool, even when he was in his '80s, he would do back flips off of the three-meter diving board. He was just this skin-and-bones kind of person—but he was so full of life that he just glowed.

After I had moved away again and worked for several decades and been through a lot of transition, I felt called to visit Ray one last time before he died.

At this point, Ray was in an elderly housing place himself. There was one in our town for the poor. He was in a room with three other men and so when I went to visit him, they sent me to his room and these three other men, I mean, they really looked like they were ready to die—all three of them. But Ray's bed was empty, so I went back to the office and asked where I could find Ray. They said something like this: "Well, he's already made his rounds today so he is probably in the quiet room."

They told me where the quiet room was and it was an interior room with a door and no windows. The door was slightly open and so I pushed it open and a voice from the dark said, "Come in, come in, come in," and I walked in and the voice again said, "Can't quite see who it is, who is it?" I said, "Rusty Meyers." Ray said, "Rusty Meyers. Well, what a pleasure, sit down." And I sat down, he began to play my life like a violin. He even told me things about myself in my early years that I had either forgotten or just didn't really know much about.

And then he said, "You know, one of the greatest days of my life was spent with you." And for the life of me, I couldn't think what he meant. He said, "It was that time we watched your son play basketball."

It happens that before my oldest son's senior year in high school, my wife and I had divorced and, since I was this prominent, upstanding citizen, complete with all the lies that I projected, which everybody thought were the truth, I was embarrassed by the divorce—it was a failure for me. And so I stopped

sitting in the reserved section with those folks and I sat in general admission and watched my son play basketball.

Basketball was big—our town was a basketball town. Unfortunately, this particular year, the two best teams in the state were in our town, so they had to have a play-off with each other to see which team would go to the state finals. So this game was standing-room only, with the fire marshal on hand to make sure nothing was wrong—you know how high school gyms are. And I was there in general admission and Ray came along and asked if he could sit beside me. It was an incredibly well-played game and my son played an incredible game—double overtime.

But now, in that small quiet room, Ray said to me, "You know, it wasn't the game that was so special, even though both teams played great and all. What made that day so special for me was that I got to sit next to a man who loved his son so much. What I remember is a father sharing his love for his son with me."

And it was true, you know. In that game, it really didn't matter whether the team won or lost. I had been humbled and was living rather humbly in those days, so to just watch my son do something was like a gift. And that was what my attitude was at moment, at that game.

Ray for me was an example of someone who was following his call.

This story hit a strong emotional cord with me on several levels. First, Ray's description of the basketball game showed that he was awake and alert to the fact that Rusty was there loving his son unconditionally regardless of the game's outcome. I couldn't help but think about my own son and how I had coached his basketball team for the past two years and had struggled with the fact that we didn't win very many games. It affirmed the idea that emptying oneself of the need to win or succeed or look good can be liberating and humbling at the same time. The important element in such activity is to practice unconditional acceptance even though one might be failing by the society's standards.

Secondly, the story of Ray is a reminder that the simplest of human activities can often be the most meaningful. This sounds like a cliche, but cliches become cliches because they contain truths. Ray seemed to be an example of someone who had become free to follow his call, and he was inner-directed enough to be able to do so and not worry about "Ray jokes" or whatever others thought of him. He was in search, not of society's definition of success or perfection, but rather, of completion and wholeness and he had the courage to pursue it. It is an inspiring story and we thank Rusty for allowing us to include it here.

Exercise: Listen for Your Call

One way to think about identifying your call—or, as Joseph Campbell says, "Follow your bliss"— is to ask yourself this: "What would I do if I could choose literally any human activity?" When you think about this, it is important to suspend for the moment the limitation of considering only those things that you believe will earn you enough money. Simply pretend that your endeavor will result in a comfortable living. Our experience is that if you can land on that which represents your deepest desire, then the money will follow. The other thing that will happen is that money no longer will be the principle objective; instead, pursuit of one's deepest desire will be the principle objective. It is also important, for the purpose of this exercise, to assume that whatever you choose will be accepted by your family, including mother, father, wife, husband, children or whichever close family relatives are impacted by your work life.

Once you have come up with an activity, flesh it out. For example, if you sit alone in a room quietly meditating on this business of your call, and what keeps surfacing is "master gardener" (just an example), then try to begin to visualize what such a career might be like. You needn't work out all the details, but it is important to be as specific as you can be about how your new career as a professional master gardener might be. Don't worry so much about how to get there. It is more important to first be very clear about the precise nature of your calling.

As I listened to Rusty describe the story of Ray, I kept making judgments (assumptions) in my mind about why a perfectly successful professor of anthropology would quit cold-turkey to become a church gardener and go visit dying people. Was he out of his mind? Was he trying to prove a point to the world?

And then I started thinking about my own career and how inauthentic politics had become and how I really concluded that I hated my job in the attorney general's office, even though on the surface it seemed like I was very successful. I began to wonder how many people are working 50 to 60 hours per week in jobs they hate, ignoring the small voice inside them calling them to authenticity and meaning.

In my own case, I began to look at those activities in which I was engaged where time itself seemed to stand still. I started to think about this after reading the book *Flow: The Psychology of Optimal Experience,* by Mihaly Csikszentmihalyi. This book reviewed the studies that have been conducted of individuals when they are in peak performance. One of the things they found is that when peak performers are "in the zone," doing what they love and are called to do, they lose track of time. I find that the only time I lose track of time is when I am either reading or writing. I will start writing a chapter and look up at the clock and it will be 8 A.M. Then, seemingly in the next instant, I look up and it says 11 A.M. . . . next it will be 2 P.M.; then 5 P.M., and the next thing I know, I will have spent 12 hours at the computer—even though it seemed like about 35 minutes.

As you think about your call, think about activities in which you have engaged in the past where hours went by before you were conscious of the time. Have you ever been engaged in something so thoroughly that time seemed no longer to be relevant? If so, it is a clue that you were doing something for which there is passion and heart and soul, and it may lead you to your call.

As you look for your call, it might feel risky and uncertain at first. It always seems more comfortable, safe even, to stick with the known, than to launch into the unknown. But the unknown is that yet-unexplored terrain where authenticity and meaning reside. In *DO IT!: Let's Get Off of Our Buts* (McWilliams and Rogers), Alan Alda put it this way:

> You have to leave the city of your comfort and go into the wilderness of your intuition. What you'll discover will be wonderful. What you'll discover will be yourself.

In addition to discerning that activity about which one is most passionate, it is also important to determine whether the activity is good for the world. Frederick Buechner, in his book *Wishful Thinking: A Seeker's ABC,* describes the process of trying to discern one's call, or purpose:

> There are all different kinds of voices calling you to do all different kinds of work, and the problem is to find out which is the voice of God, rather than that of

> society, say, or the superego, or self-interest. By and large, a good rule for finding this out is the following: The kind of work God usually calls you to is the kind of work (a) that you need most to do, and (b) that the world needs most to have done. If you really get a kick out of your work, you've presumably met requirement (a) but if your work is writing deodorant commercials, the chances are, you've missed requirement (b).
>
> On the other hand, if your work is being a physician in a leper colony, you've probably met requirement (b) but if most of the time you're bored and depressed by your work, the chances are that you've not only bypassed (a), but probably aren't helping your patients much either. Neither the hair shirt nor the soft berth will do. The place God calls you to is the place where your deep gladness and the world's deep hunger meet.

The place where your deep gladness and the world's deep hunger meet is the essential authentic self. It is the source of satisfaction in work and life for the individual, it is the source of hope for a troubled world and it is the stable ground of being, which is effected by neither time nor space. Ray discovered that being with people before they die was the place where his deep gladness met one of the world's deep hungers and so he gave up all the trappings, as well as the rewards, of prestige and fame and popularity, in order to pursue an authentic life. Did he lead a more meaningful, content life than others? I think if Ray could answer that question, he would say something like, "I don't know if my life was good or bad—I was just following my call."

Too often we ignore the still, small voice of wisdom that has always known our call. LISTEN TO IT, TRUST IT, FOLLOW IT. Another one of Rusty Meyers's teachers was a native

American elder named Pete Catches. Toward the end of Pete's life, he gave Rusty a challenge that Rusty continues to hold to this day and attempts to practice. It may just apply to us all:

It's not about anything you know
or anything you don't know.
It's not about anything you will learn
or you won't learn.
It's about trust,
It's about faith.
You must always follow your call.
Never believe you're doing it,
have no attachment to outcome,
and seek no return.

—Pete Catches

Recommended Reading:

Csikszentmihalyi, Mihaly. 1990. *Flow: The Psychology of Optimal Experience.* New York: Harper & Row, Publishers.

Hillman, James. 1996. *The Soul's Code: In Search of Character and Calling.* New York: Random House.

McWilliams, Peter, and Rogers, John. 1991. *DO IT!: Let's Get Off Our Buts.* Los Angeles: Prelude Press.

Nietzche, Frederick. Kaufman, Walter, trans. 1954. *Thus Spoke Zarathustra: A Book for None and All.* New York: Penguin Books.

Chapter Eleven

Finding Your Own Islands of Acceptance

Life is either a daring adventure, or nothing.
Security does not exist in nature,
nor do the children of God
as a whole experience it.
Avoiding danger is no safer in the long run
than exposure.

—Helen Keller

HAVING SPENT THE PAST THREE YEARS STUDYING THE IMPACT OF participation in groups and community-building workshops on individuals, we have obviously concluded that such participation can be of enormous value as individuals pursue the road of healing and wholeness. One word of caution is in order. Even though we have referred to groups as "islands of acceptance" in this book, it is important to understand what we mean by that. When we say groups are like islands of acceptance, that does not mean that they are islands of safety.

As Helen Keller aptly puts it, there is no such thing as safety and in some ways, it is an act of courage to reach out to others in pursuit of the truth. Most of the transformations we have reported in this book have been the result of individuals bravely removing the psychological defenses that in some cases have been in place for decades, and uncovering previously-suppressed emotions and feelings that have been a deterrent to their spiritual and psychological growth.

In this chapter, we want to give you thoughts from some of the people who lead groups, and also encourage you to link up with groups that may exist in your community, so that you can continue to learn and practice acceptance.

Group Leaders Speak of Words

Bill Thatcher: At a meeting of FCE leaders and workshop facilitators in October 1996, one day was spent considering words that we all felt were descriptive of key aspects of community building; toward the latter part of the day, people wrote their thoughts about the concepts we had discussed. Here are some excerpts taken from their written comments:

Listening (Ann Hoewing):

I recently heard a Fortune 500 corporation representative observe that their employees operated out of two communication modes—talking and waiting to talk. Neither of these has much to do with listening. I don't feel I am over-generalizing when I say that this observation accurately reflects our culture.

Before my training with FCE I had taken and taught many communication courses and seminars. It was only through FCE's community-building process that I experienced listening attentively and being listened to attentively. I actually learned how to listen attentively—an important distinction, because it adds a dimension of consciousness and intention to listening.

What I currently find fascinating to facilitate as well as to observe is the emergence of wisdom from deep group listening. I now have a fuller understanding about what total participation means—total listening as every member. I wonder what would/will be possible if only this principle would be widely practiced. My belief is the seemingly simple principles of speaking from one's own experience and attentive listening could do much to transform ourselves and our world.

Openness to the Spirit (Gini Grace):

> ***The jump is so frightening***
> ***Between where I am and***
> ***where I want to be . . .***
> ***Because of all I may become***
> ***I will close my eyes and leap.***
>
> *—Maryanne Radmacher Hershey*

I have learned that in order to be open to something new I have to be willing to empty myself of the old. Or, to put it another way, in order to learn something I don't know, I have to be willing to be empty of what I do know. Emptiness precedes openness.

Risk and the Spirit (Vicki Lehning):

One of the dictionary definitions of principles includes, "An instinct . . . or natural tendency." For me, the principles of community building come in every form except naturally. When I look at FCE's list of principles, I can readily accept their value. On a day that hasn't challenged me too much, I might even be able to rationalize that, for the most part, I "naturally" operate out

of these principles. But the truth is that in order to be authentic, to really remove my mask and welcome the unknown, I must consciously and intentionally resist the instincts with which I've become familiar—the ones that say, "Don't rock the boat; don't dig too deep; don't cry; don't offend, and only hang out with people whose instincts determine that they'll be this polite, too."

The times I've made the leap of faith into that sacred place of risk have been God-given. The rewards have been joyful beyond what the safe, non-risk-taking version of me could have imagined.

Reliance On the Spirit (Robert Reusing):

Let me first say that I'm still not sure what is the definition of a principle. I do know that to facilitate in community building it is essential to rely on the Spirit beyond ourselves. I like to think of this as acting from my fullness or as Indigenous people speak about "original medicine."

I see two problems with stating "reliance on the Spirit" as a principle in this work. One is how do I know it is the Spirit and not ego and the other problem concerns people who do not believe in the Spirit.

One can usually feel when it is the Spirit acting. I don't believe it is enough, however, to rely on one's feelings. The spiritual voice needs to be checked out by community. As a human being I have many blind spots. Left to my own devices I may not always interpret correctly my "original medicine" or, as the Quakers say, that still small voice within. It needs to be checked out with the community.

I believe in community we can do the same for people who have a problem with the Spirit beyond themselves. The community itself needs a critical mass of people who believe in a Higher Power.

The Spirit as a Moving Force (Lyman Randall):

I believe the first-century-writer Saint Paul described the Spirit as being similar to the wind: Where it comes from and where it goes we do not really know. All that we can say is that the Spirit is a moving force (like the wind).

Using the wind/Spirit metaphor, we might visualize ourselves as a kite. To be lifted or moved by the wind, a kite must be exposed to it; the kite must be outside, in the elements of the outdoors. The kite will never fly if it remains "safe" indoors. Even when outdoors, there are days or times when no wind comes, and the kite will remain dormant. The wind cannot be commanded. It just IS as it IS.

Emptiness (Janice Barfield):

I believe emptiness is one of the most important—if not the most important—principles in community. Emptying implies that something was held—or contained—before the opposite occurred. At the beginning of community building, we hold ideas, prejudices and judgments that are antithetical to community. It is important that these ideas and even judgments are brought into the open—if not verbally, then certainly recognized within ourselves.

Emptying nearly always involves the element of surprise for me. When I truly "empty" myself of my preconceptions, of what I think I know, I am sometimes horrified at what comes forth. Afterward, I am almost always relieved.

Balance (Jonathan Lange):

I've been thinking lately in terms of three. It seems to me that the idea of paradox—the tension or balance between two

things which are contradictory but true—does not go far enough when it comes to community/emptiness. Most great truths come in threes: Body, Mind & Spirit; Earth, Fire & Water; Faith, Hope & Love. Even "being in the present" is not simply a matter of being midway between the Past and the Future. All three are places or attitudes unto themselves. The philosopher Hegel developed the idea of dialectic: moving from thesis to antithesis and then resolving the tension with synthesis. But, it seems to me that all those three are different and have their own pull.

So what I suggest is that living from emptiness or being in community is staying in the middle of, being in reference to, three things rather than two. Living or balancing in the very midst of three realities which are equally significant yet very different.

Silence (Patrick Lima):

In community building, silence is indeed golden—a starting point—a state that is paradoxically both private and shared, individual and common. Silence is fertile. Apparently a blank space, it is the void—like the void at the dawn of creation—into which, out of which, something new and creative comes—is breathed.

Silence is spacious. It invites us—challenges us—to speak and somehow we speak in a different way when we are aware of breaking the silence than we do in ordinary non-stop banter.

Out in the wider world, silence is rare. But when we want to honor, pay homage and remember those fallen in wars, those killed in ways that are blatantly untimely, unfair and shocking, we have a minute of silence. Their is a shared sense that silence is precious and can be memory-full.

In silence, in the eye of the storm, we may catch a whisper of One who speaks not in the thunder, or in the whirlwind but in a still small voice—of love.

Tolerating Ambiguity (Jo Ann Bobbitt):

Realizing that I have the capacity to be a vessel or container to hold differing opinions, values, and perceptions along with my own does not come naturally. This requires a level of consciousness that takes work like any new skill. The community-building model offers the opportunity to learn and experience tölerating ambiguity as a way to relate with others in our world.

The experience of first recognizing and then removing the log from my own eyes allows space to hold others while they remove the splinter from their eye. This holding creates an environment where the energy otherwise used to defend, justify, and prove one's rightness can then be utilized for healthy processing.

Holding On and Letting Go (Ellen Stephen):

The concept of "holding on" relates to the characteristics of integrity and commitment. It also involves courage and moral strength. Inevitably, this brings up a need for discernment: What are we to hold on to? I have sometimes used the image of a deciduous tree to illustrate the difficulties of this discernment. The pitfall of holding on for too long would be like catching autumn leaves and trying to staple them back onto their branches. The opposite pitfall would be not only to let the leaves fall and prune away dead growth, but to hack off so much live wood that the sap would run out and the tree would die. In FCE culture, "letting go" involves the characteristic of risking, being vulnerable—submitting to something greater than self. I think there may be four aspects of letting go:

First, there is the letting go of one's biases and pre-judgments in order to truly listen in the moment. A second aspect is respectful listening. This is the appropriate emptying or bracketing of one's own agenda to make space for that of another—

an individual or group. Third, there is letting go of the need to control. This touches upon the hard discipline of letting go of my rights, in appropriate instances, and even perhaps of my sense of righteousness. And, fourth, this opens up the whole subject of surrendering. Alcoholics Anonymous speaks of "surrendering to one's higher power." Closely related to this is the idea of "submission to something greater than self." This may be seen as taking the principle of letting go to its fullest extent.

Letting go must be done by choice, not coercion. The one who let's go and surrenders becomes a benefactor.

Fear and Protection (Bonnie Poindexter):

Awareness of the tension between holding on and letting go is perhaps the greatest of the principles for me. This principle could be translated to the AA's "Let go and let God." This idea is made powerful in the community-building model during the experiential time in the circle that demonstrates the way emptiness can bring the understanding needed to reduce the fear of letting go. The example that comes to mind is jumping out of an airplane. The time between leaving the plane and the chute opening is for me a definition of how fearful it is to LET GO. No wonder people don't want to subject themselves to this kind of learning. It is far too scary. How can I convey to the people in my life who are frightened that they can be held and protected by the group while they jump—much as we are held in the arms of a loving and compassionate God?

Open-Hearted, Open-Minded (Mary Ann Schmidt):

It is a reality that life on planet earth is diverse. There are different cultures, different religions, different viewpoints on how to do and be practically anything. To achieve the goal of peaceful creative living (which it is my assumption that most of us want), it is necessary to realize that one's own point of view—on anything—is simply one way to look at it. In fact the limitations of acting only on one's "own piece of the elephant" contribute to our deepest problems in that inevitably a single-minded solution solves one problem and probably creates another. In community building or in working toward a sustainable future, it is essential for each person to actively work at achieving an open mind—and particularly an open heart.

A Group of All Leaders (Garry Eldridge):

One of the basic principles of community is that it is a group of all leaders. As a group of all leaders, each individual who is a part of the community accepts and shares responsibility for the group. While a community will likely have designated leaders or facilitators, these individuals are not the center of responsibility for the group. In community, each and every individual has responsibility for the successes, failures, norms, culture, rituals, policies, weaknesses, strengths, decisions, values, development, growth, changes, etc., of the group as a whole.

It is not difficult to see why most groups are not communities, and do not function in and out of community. Most individuals do not want to accept the level of responsibility implied in the principle that a community is a group of all leaders. Many individuals are lazy about responsibility, and would rather let someone else worry about it. Many individuals would rather not be blamed for the failures or weaknesses in their group. While they might be willing to share in the successes of the group, they are more likely to avoid accepting personal responsibility for the group to avoid accepting blame or failure.

When a group chooses to function from the principle that it is a group of all leaders, the level of individual and corporate investment in the group increases. If I accept my role as a leader in a group of all leaders, then I want the group's work to succeed and will, in turn, invest myself and energy into bringing it to fruition.

In a group of all leaders, the voice of each individual is valued and given serious consideration. This means that even the dissenting voice—even the voice standing alone in the midst of the group—is heard and taken seriously. Therefore, for a group to be this kind of community, a fundamental shift in thinking is required for the designated leader(s) and for the designated follower(s).

Leading by Example (Eve Berry):

The principle of leading by example is one fundamental aspect of FCE's work. Our mission statement refers to "living, learning and teaching the principles of community." As people experience community building and "discover new ways of being together," the most basic application of these learnings back home is to put in practice the principles of community. But is the act of "living . . . the principles of community" a principle? I believe it is. Perhaps it is even a "meta-principle," or a principle that stands behind and forms a backdrop for other principles.

Mahatma Gandhi articulated the spirit of the principle so well when he said, "Be the change you want to see in the world." If we are to change the world using the principles of community as a pathway, the change starts from within oneself and spreads from there. We also see this principle of leading by example at work in the story "The Rabbi's Gift," which

is used to begin community-building workshops. The aura of deep respect that surrounded the old monks in the story would not have been felt had they not put the principle of respect into practice.

Perhaps the most compelling rationale for the importance of leading by example as an FCE principle is its alignment with leading-edge research in the "new sciences." Physicist David Bohm proposed that we live in a holographic universe in which every part of the universe both contains and contributes to the whole. If one part is affected by something, i.e., some change, it affects the whole and vice versa. Given this emerging perspective on the nature of reality, it really does make a difference whether or not each of us chooses to live, learn and teach the principles of community.

Relate with Love, Respect and Acceptance (Margaret MacCormack):

There is an example from a recent community-building workshop that helps illustrate the significance of acceptance through love and respect:

A well-educated, although somewhat naive, woman about 40 years old came to her first workshop. She had had many psychological problems and had enrolled in, or organized, several different groups in the past. She was a difficult person to accommodate in the workshop. She demanded a large share of attention from participants, and used various manipulative methods to get it. People began to resent her over-use of "air time," and said so, sometimes strongly. Others tried to listen with empathy. At one point, the group was surprised to hear she had left the workshop, to return, just as unexpectedly, the following day. During her absence, she became, even more, the

center of attention than before. Participants regretted having failed to support her needs. It was as if she became the group's "task," which eventually was what brought the group into community, while she was gone. When she returned, the group was ready to respond to her, as a group.

I have tried to look at what the community-building group did. Did they give her advice? No need for that. She had lists of contacts with therapists of all kinds and was familiar with a host of reports and books about new practices and theories.

Did they scold her for childish behavior or try to persuade her how her stories were just fantasies? Some must have. Others lost patience with her, for the same reasons. The result of these tactics seemed to bring out even more bizarre behavior and unbelievable stories, because she felt attacked. What did make a difference, however, was the people who listened with full attention and tried to hear her stories the way she felt them, transmitting to her that she was being taken seriously.

About six weeks after the workshop, she discovered that she had an advanced cancer—a shock to herself and, as word spread, a cause for unease among those who felt that, maybe, they hadn't taken her seriously enough. Some visited her when she was later hospitalized. Her manner during these visits showed evidence of inner transformation. Though seriously ill, she now spoke in well-grounded terms with no trace of the improbable-sounding fantasies. She was interested in other people, and it was enjoyable to spend time with her. Visitors were hearing from her true self. She said to her family, "This group, these people who don't even know me, are the first people who have ever accepted me as I am. She died only four months from that workshop, having experienced very briefly the knowledge that she was accepted and the profound sense of self-validation it gave.

The Fear of Transformation

Doug Shadel: We stifle our emotions and feelings for a good reason: they often represent pain. But if you remember anything at all from this book, remember this: the pain is there whether you sweep it under the carpet or not. As Carl Jung has said, "Neurosis is always a substitute for legitimate suffering." It is when we avoid pain that we run the risk of it having the greatest negative effect on us. The best way to deal with life's suffering is to surface it and allow others to carry it with you.

The Outward Bound people have a saying:

If you can't get out of it, get into it.

There is no getting out of reality and reality from time to time involves pain. At the end of this chapter are places you can contact in order to link up with groups in your community. I have a personal reason for listing these self-help resources and making them available here. I have had three close relatives die at early ages (ages 40, 55 and 63, respectively) in my lifetime. One committed suicide, another died of complications related to HIV and a third died of prostate cancer. But what they all really died from was the steadfast refusal to ask for help. And this determined refusal takes us all the way back to the beginning chapter on the culture of rugged individualism.

All three of these individuals were smart enough to know they needed help but were afraid to ask for it. They were, like me, so thoroughly entrenched in the culture of rugged individualism that they felt it simply was not an option to acknowledge "need" to anyone! All three of these relatives of mine died from rugged individualism.

I described in Chapter One how I, too, was headed along the path of rugged individualism until I realized it just wasn't working. I have since joined several groups, gotten therapy and become a huge advocate of group membership. So for all of the card-carrying rugged individualists out there, if I can do it, so can you. Joining a group is not a sign of being a wimp or a show of weakness. In fact, paradoxically, I have never felt more in control of my life than I do right now, having surrendered the idea (the lie) that I was invincible.

No one is invincible and those who think they are deceive themselves. This is why the first step in twelve-step programs is for people to give up the belief that they are in control. It is also why Ernest Kurst, in writing about the history of Alcoholics Anonymous, titled his book *Not-God.* Even though we are taught from an early age that the goal is to gain as much control and power as we can, ultimately this is an illusion. And you don't need to be an alcoholic or a batterer or have some other condition that, while very real, tends to stereotype the self-help movement itself.

I find joining a support group to be a sign of an inner-directed, fully-functioning human being— like a wheel rolling out of its own center—who is determined to continually move toward health and wholeness and away from isolation and disconnection. And to those who say that support groups do not represent true community, we say anything that will help move a person toward self-acceptance and healing is worth doing.

The principle struggle many people go through is the transition from a former way of being to a new way of being. In *Warriors of the Heart,* Danaan Perry says:

> Sometimes I feel that my life is a series of trapeze swings. I'm either hanging on to a trapeze bar swinging along or for a few moments in my life, I'm hurtling across space in between trapeze bars.

Most of the time, I spend my life hanging on for dear life to my trapeze-bar-of-the-moment. It carries me along at a certain steady rate of swing and I have the feeling that I'm in control of my life. I know most of the right questions and even some of the right answers. But once in a while, as I'm merrily (or not-so-merrily) swinging along, I look out ahead of me into the distance and what do I see? I see another trapeze bar swinging toward me. Its empty, and I know in that place in me that knows, that this "new trapeze bar" has my name on it. It is my next step, my growth, my aliveness coming to get me. In my heart-of-hearts I know that for me to grow, I must release my grip on the present, well-known bar to move to the new one.

Each time it happens to me, I hope (no, I pray) that I won't have to grab the new one. But in my knowing place I know that I must totally release my grasp on my old bar and for some moment in time I must hurtle across space before I can grab onto the new bar. Each time I am filled with terror. It doesn't matter that in all my previous hurtles across the void of knowing I have always made it. Each time I am afraid that I will miss, that I will be crushed on the unseen rocks in the bottomless chasm between the bars. But I do it anyway. Perhaps this is the essence of what the mystics call the faith experience. No guarantees, no net, no insurance policy. But you do it anyway because somehow to keep hanging on to that old bar is no longer on the list of possible alternatives.

And so for an eternity that can last a microsecond or a thousand lifetimes, I soar across the dark void of "the past is gone, the future is not yet here." It is called transition. I have come to believe that is the only place where real change occurs. I mean real change. Not the pseudo-change that only lasts until the next time my old buttons get pushed.

I have noticed that, in our culture, this transition zone is looked upon as a "no-thing," a "no-place" between places. Sure, the old trapeze bar was real, and that new one coming toward me, I hope that's real too. But the void between? That's just a scary, confusing, disorienting "nowhere" that must be gotten through as fast and as unconsciously as possible. What a waste! I have a sneaking suspicion that the transition zone is the only real thing, and the bars are illusions we dream up to avoid the void, where the real change, the real growth occurs for us. Whether or not my hunch is true, it remains that the transition zones in our lives are incredibly rich places. They should be honored, even savored. Yes, with all the pain and fear and feelings of being out-of-control that can (but not necessarily) accompany transitions, they are still the most alive, most growth-filled, passionate, expansive moments in our lives.

There are countless organizations that can help you find others seeking to make the transition between trapeze bars. Whether you decide to join an existing group or start your own, the important thing is to make that first phone call. Think of the call as your next leap of faith, across to the next trapeze.

The following are organizations you can contact in order to discover other people who are seeking islands of acceptance, or to learn how to create your own group.

INTERNATIONAL

Foundation for Community Encouragement
P.O. Box 17210
Seattle, WA 98107
(206) 784-9000
Fax: (206) 784-9077
Helps individuals and organizations learn how to build and sustain community. Offers community-building experiences, workshops, skills seminars and conferences to the general public. Also develops custom-designed programs for organizations, nonprofit and for-profit.

NATIONAL

American Self-Help Clearinghouse
57 Clares-Riverside Medical Center
Denville, NJ 07834
(201) 625-7101
Provides information on and referrals to national self-help groups and local self-help clearinghouses. Publishes The Self-Help Sourcebook.

National Mental Health Consumers' Self-Help Clearinghouse
1211 Chestnut Street
Philadelphia, PA 19107-4103
(800) 553-4KEY
Fax: (215) 636-6310
Consumer self-help resource information geared toward meeting individual and group needs regarding mental health. Assistance in advocacy, listings of publications, training, on-site consultations, educational events. Funded by the Center of Mental Health Services.

National Self-Help Clearinghouse
25 West 43rd Street
New York, NY 10036.
Publishes the Self-Help Reporter *and many other educational materials. Send a self-addressed stamped envelope to receive information.*

Recommended Reading:

Parry, Danaan. 1991. *Warriors of the Heart: A Handbook for Conflict Resolution.* Cooperstown, N.Y.: Sunstone Publications.

CHAPTER TWELVE

The Principles of Acceptance

The Stoics say:
"Withdraw into yourself—
that is where you will find peace."
And that is not true. Others say:
"Go outside: look for happiness in some diversion." And
that is not true: we may fall sick.
Happiness is neither outside nor inside us:
it is in God, both outside and inside us.

—Blaise Pascal

WE SET OUT TO STUDY THE GROUP WORKSHOP PROCESS USING THE example of the community-building workshops primarily because they have so thoroughly transformed both of us. Doug moved from the rugged individual described in Chapter One who dealt only with individuals with whom he could cut deals and advance his career to the youth basketball coach, theology/psychology student and counselor. As such he feels like a tadpole who has newly developed lungs but is not yet comfortable breathing through them. Bill's journey was a bit different. In Chapter Seven he described how he found in community building a framework that provided integration for more intentional living and an opportunity, through facilitating workshops, to become a freedom fighter in the quest for community.

The starting point for our joint journey, which has produced this book, was a mutual desire to explore both the impact and implications of making community building a way of life. We've selfishly done this for ourselves. The interviews with workshop participants conducted over the last two years have touched us deeply. We have met "traveling companions" who have helped us on our own journey of discovery. Their voices strike a resounding chord that lifts us up and encourages us onward. They are our heroes.

What has emerged for us are some principles that we believe speak to human existence and the barriers to connection and meaning individuals experience on a daily basis. These principles reflect both paradox and simplicity, they call forth the gifts with which we are blessed and reveal our shadowed road to health and wholeness. The sobering news is that no one can walk this road for us. The good news is that we are invited to walk it with others.

It may be apparent that throughout this book, we have focused on particular words, and then provided insights about them, gained from the community-building study and the experiences of dozens of other people who have participated in a variety of experiential learning models.

Below are seven "principles" of acceptance. For each word, we provide a summary of some of the insights we gained from this two-year study of community building, and some meditations that you may find useful in beginning to embody some of these principles.

One strong caveat is in order. We believe the process of personal growth, transformation and living in the world is distinctly unique for each individual. This is what makes life so vibrant, interesting and even mysterious. It also means it is impossible to arrive at anything resembling a definitive list of "ways of being" or "keys to success" or "action steps to a better you." Both of us dislike such seemingly finite approaches because they presuppose that we know precisely what it is like to live in the world as another person. In fact, it presupposes that we know exactly what it is like to live in the world as most people. Neither is true.

The principles listed here are offered as signposts along the road that we have come to find meaningful as we interviewed folks and studied the community-building model. We do not suggest that these principles represent the only road signs to acceptance. There are many, and only you can choose the ones that are right for you.

THESE PRINCIPLES ARE:

1. Emptiness
2. Openness
3. Unconditionality
4. Empathy
5. Inner-directedness
6. Congruence
7. Purposefulness

1. The Principle of Emptiness

We have said that the most important stage of community building is called "emptiness." The goal of a workshop is to bring a group to the point where they have emptied themselves of the need to fix, control, blame, judge or persuade others. Once a critical mass of participants has reached this stage, it allows room for community to emerge.

We have seen how individuals report that going through such a process increases their feeling of connectedness to many of those around them. For once they have emptied themselves of what amount to barriers to connecting with others, they are freer to choose to connect.

There is a great story that illustrates the importance of emptiness. A professor of Eastern religion had spent his entire professional life studying the philosophy of a great religious leader and mystic in India. Toward the end of his career he was given the opportunity, while on sabbatical, to visit with this great master. When the time came, he and the master sat down and the professor began by telling the master how anxious he was to learn from him and how he had read all of his writings and considered him to be one of the great mystics of our time.

In the meantime, the master had asked the American professor if he would like some tea. The professor said yes and while he continued to talk, the master poured his tea. As the professor kept talking, the master kept pouring until the tea cup was running over. The professor finally noticed that the tea was spilling out onto the table and onto the floor and he said, "What are you doing?" The master sat calmly and silently for a moment and then said, "Just as the tea cup is full and can receive no more tea, so, too, are you so filled with information that it would be impossible for you to learn anything from me."

In order to receive, we must make room. If we continue to fill up with the culture of materialism and the zero-sum competitiveness that pervades our minds, and continue to ignore the human spirit, we are, in effect, telling God there is no room at the inn:

> On their travels, tourists seeking accommodations watch for the "Vacancy" sign outside motels. Dismay sets in when, one after the other, all they see is the cruel "No Vacancy" message, which happy proprietors switch on

> when every room is filled. This image reflects. . .when life is cluttered with excessive activity, glutted with material possession, or flooded with spiritual gifts or a multitude of relationships, it can well happen that the consumption of time and energy is so great that the mystery of God is shelved, if not forgotten. There is simply no inner space left and the divine Guest remains at the door, facing the blinking "No Vacancy" sign. Matters of the spirit are thus ignored or neglected.
>
> —ROBERT F. MORNEAU *(SPIRITUAL DIRECTION)*

If we are to welcome the spirit and therefore the assistance it can bring, we must be intentional about emptying and making room for it.

We have mentioned that community-building participants reported experiencing an increased connectedness to God as a result of their participation (see Chapter Five). Why?

In 1991, Walter Wink, who is a professor of New Testament at Auburn Theological Seminary and has written numerous scholarly books on the New Testament, wrote a review of M. Scott Peck's work in *Theology Today* magazine. Among his criticisms of Peck's work was the idea proposed by Peck in *The Road Less Traveled* that we are called to Godhood, to become God. Wink was referring to the following passage from *The Road Less Traveled:*

> For no matter how much we may like to pussyfoot around it, all of us who postulate a loving God and really think about it eventually come to a single terrifying idea: God wants us to become Himself (or Herself or Itself). We are growing toward Godhood. God is the goal of evolution.

Wink criticized this statement since it does not distinquish between "relating to" or "knowing" God versus "becoming" God. Wink suggests that the danger of implying the goal is to become God is that it may encourage idolatry.

Peck then submitted a fascinating response to this criticism that elucidates for us his vision of the concept of emptiness and one way to view our relationship with God or spirit. (Peck's response also appeared in *Theology Today,* in the October 1991 edition) It reads in part:

> Probably nothing has given readers more theological indigestion in *The Road Less Traveled* than the notion that we humans are called to become God (didn't Satan set himself up as God?). Even so, it is not necessarily a heresy, being standard doctrine in the Orthodox church, known as the doctrine of the "deification of man." . . . Were I to rewrite *The Road Less Traveled,* I would not drop the doctrine, but I would add something like: "But there is a paradox here, and that is that we, ourselves, cannot become God except by bumping ourselves off. The process is one that real theologians refer to as "kenosis"—the process of self-emptying. The goal is imaged by that of the empty vessel, in which there is still enough ego left to comprise the walls of the vessel, but which is otherwise sufficiently empty to be able to become spirit-filled.

While the community-building model is not religiously based, the principle of emptiness does have a spiritual foundation. If we are to begin to practice acceptance as a means of moving closer to the truth, it must begin with kenosis, or self-emptying. We must intentionally "make room" for the other, whether it is knowledge or spirit or God, so that we can move forward toward wholeness or completion. And in so doing we will find that the world will present itself to us.

Sometimes individuals grow weary waiting for God to act while, ironically, God is waiting for them to let go of an inordinate attachment and surrender to God in trust."

—Philip L. Boroughs
(Fleming, ed., Ministry of Spiritual Directorn*)*

Meditation for embodying the principle of emptiness:

Today I will empty myself of those things that get in the way of inviting the spirit to participate in the act of co-creating with me.

2. The Principle of Openness

Cultivating a sense of "openness" to all of the experiences going on around us is vital to personal growth and development. As we have described over and over in this book, it is the surfacing and experiencing of emotions, some of which can be painful, that neutralizes their damaging effects. The more one is open to what's going on for them, the better able they are to deal with it. So much of the time we close down and shut off what is going on as a remedy against the pain we fear such experiences will cause, only to find out later that the "medicine" did more harm than the disease. Part of accepting oneself is accepting the authentic experiencing that occurs rather than covering it up in order to acquire acceptance from others.

Being open to experience can also facilitate connection with God. Paul Tillich said that, as a professional theologian, the most common question he was asked was, "What can I do to experience God or to get the Divine Spirit? His answer was, "The only thing you can do is keep yourselves open. You cannot force God down, you cannot produce the Divine Spirit in yourselves, but what you can do is open yourselves—keep yourself open for it." (Rogers, *Dialogues*).

Whether it is openness to spirit or to authentic emotions or feelings, the important point is to run toward experience and not away from it. As Donald Nichol has said, "We cannot fail once we realize that everything that happens to us is designed to teach us holiness." If this is true, that every single experience we have is designed to teach us how to move in the direction of holiness or healing, then we have a significant incentive to remain open to such experiencing.

Meditation for embodying the principle of Openness:

I will openly and enthusiastically accept and experience
all of my emotions and feelings
as they occur today.
I will also remain open to the experience of others.

3. The Principle of Unconditionality

There is a yearning within each of us for unconditional acceptance. But from our earliest moments of conscious human relationships, we are led to believe that <u>conditional</u> acceptance can be just as satisfying. It's a lie.

We believe the road to acceptance in all of its manifestations often can begin with the concept of unconditionality. This is defined as the refusal to set conditions on oneself and others in order to gain acceptance.

Unconditionality is directly related to the principle of emptiness in that what one often is trying to empty oneself of are conditions upon which contentment is based. "If I could just get a raise" or "if my wife would just listen to me" or "if I could just make more money per month" or "if I could only get my son to cut his hair and sit up straight at the table," then I would be happy.

This principle can seem counter-intuitive on its face because in our competitive world, we are taught to set conditions and standards for ourselves in order to move up the ladder of success and gain acceptance. But how can I do that if I am supposed to empty myself of all conditions? The dilemma of when to hold on and when to let go has plagued Doug for years. He has asked ES this question numerous times during the past several years.

The question is "If I am already unconditionally accepted by a loving God, then why do anything?" Why not just sit around on the couch with the channel changer all day? Furthermore, as the bible reminds us, God is no respecter of persons, meaning God does not acknowledge worldly status and achievement as a condition of acceptance. If that is true, then why bother?

After months of probing ES about this, she was able to provide a way of thinking about it that clicked for Doug. In response to the question, "If I am already accepted, why do anything?" she said:

Because just as light must shine
and fire must burn, love must act.

(The Rule of the Anglican Order
of the Holy Cross)

Oh! Never mind—I get it now. Her point was that good action is not done for the purpose of adding to some divine resume that one presents upon entrance into heaven. Rather, emptying oneself of conditions that are often existential in nature and not based in divine love, can facilitate getting in touch with one's authentic calling and allow love to surface. It is love, not the need for status, which should compel action.

Those conditions, then, with which we fill ourselves in the existential world to gain status, short of getting us closer to acceptance, can actually move us further from it to the extent it is not in pursuit of what we are truly called to do.

As we mentioned in the section on The Principle of Emptiness, one of the profound learnings we took away from our study of community-building workshops is that individuals report a closer connection to God (as they understand it) as a result of their participation. We believe, as we have implied in previous chapters, that it is the emptying of conditions such as the need to convert or fix or heal or control that makes room for authentic connection with the spirit and allows participants to move closer to having an authentic relationship with that spirit.

The fact that these same participants reported that they felt better able to live more authentically as well is consistent with our theory of the effects of emptying on behavior. If one can, even for a short time, become free from the clutter and noise and expectations of modern life, one can connect with a higher power and begin to more clearly discern one's calling. Or, to paraphrase ES, they can begin to "let love act" as ultimately it must.

Meditation for embodying the principle of unconditionality:

Today I accept the way I am, the way others are
and the way the world is and I will not place
conditions on accepting myself or others.

4. The Principle of Inner-Directedness

This principle of acceptance is closely related to unconditionality. Becoming free from the need for external reinforcement enables us to look inward for acceptance and to begin to act more authentically. And, paradoxically, as we become less and less dependent on the opinions of others, we can become increasingly close to and connected with those same others as a deliberate choice.

Remember that separation must precede and coexist with connection in order for the connection to be authentic and based on free choice. We found compelling evidence that participation in community building workshops and/or support groups decreased the importance participants place on the opinions of others (see Chapter Four). Contemporaneously, they experienced increased feelings of connectedness to most everyone in their lives.

The "thou shalts" to which Nietzsche referred in *Thus Spoke Zaranthustra* are relevant here. How many "thou shalts" do you still carry around that must be met in order to feel accepted? One way to begin to discern this is to list them. Take out a piece of paper and a pencil and begin to list the things that you feel you absolutely must do in your life as it is now in order to gain acceptance. The "thou shalts" can be as simple as feeling the need to wear the latest fashion or being at a certain weight so you can look like the super models on television.

"Thou-shalt" messages run ceaselessly throughout our culture, promising to fill that deep longing for unconditional acceptance with possessions, experiences, or social standing. The half truth is they fill us up but they do not satisfy. It is like a person invited to the best restaurant in town who, before being allowed to feast, is first required to fill up with water.

C.S. Lewis addresses this point in *Mere Christianity.* He writes:

> People often think of Christian morality as a kind of bargain in which God says, "If you keep a lot of rules, I'll

> reward you, and if you don't, I'll do the other thing." I do not think that is the best way of looking at it. I would much rather say that every time you make a choice you are turning the central part of you, the part of you that chooses, into something a little different from what it was before. And taking your life as a whole, with all your innumerable choices, all your life long you are slowly turning this central thing into a Heaven creature or into a hellish creature: either into a creature that is in harmony with God, and with other creatures, and with itself, or else into one that is in a state of war and hatred with God, and with its fellow creatures, and with itself. To be the one kind of creature is Heaven: that is, it is joy, and peace, and knowledge, and power. To be the other means madness, horror, idiocy, rage, impotence, and eternal loneliness. Each of us at each moment is progressing to the one state or the other.

By choosing to look within for direction, the inner-directed person can experience a kind of freedom that does not exist for most of us in this conditional love world. Free from the fleeting and arbitrary whims of a culture dominated by excess and materialism, one can move closer and closer to that which is transcendent, unchanging and, most importantly, true. The truth about the glory of what it means to be human cannot be found by getting a view office, a hot new car and a big house. And yet many of us spend a majority of our time pursuing such material go(o)ds.

> If we are to find true glory, we must first look for it and secondly choose it.
>
> Because we come out of the divine nature, which chooses to be divine, we must choose to be divine, to be

> of God, to be one with God, loving and living as he loves and lives, and so be partakers of the divine nature, or we perish. Man cannot originate this life; it must be shown him, and he must choose it.
>
> —GEORGE MACDONALD (*CREATION IN CHRIST*)

The community-building workshops in which we have participated have provided us with the courage we need to move in the direction of choosing to be more inner-directed, people who remember that we are already unconditionally accepted and that the real task of personal and spiritual growth is to build an ever stronger link with God. The consequence can be to have a clearer picture of why we are here and where we should go.

By affirming that who we are is enough, we are free to be who we are without carrying the tremendous burden of continually having to prove it to the outside world. A word of caution about beginning to embody the principle of inner-directedness. As we mentioned earlier, the paradox is that there is nothing that can generate both respect and anger more than a truly inner-directed person.

To live this way, one must have a strong community in which to derive ongoing support for risking living the authentic life. Otherwise, it can be a pretty lonely and precarious existence. This is one of the reasons we have provided resource phone numbers in this book for you to call depending on where you live so that you can either hook up with an existing group or start your own.

In order to sail the seas of public opinion under your own power, not using the winds of popular culture, you must never be too far from an island of acceptance, a port of safety into which you can retreat to rest and be nurtured. Without it, you risk being battered and destroyed at sea.

Meditation for embodying the principle of inner-directedness:

Today I will focus my attention on connection with my higher power and inner wisdom and seek internal guidance for how to interact in the world.

5. The Principle of Empathy

One of the characteristics of an effective therapist is to have genuine empathy for the patient. This means as much as possible to try to put yourself in the shoes of the person with whom you are interacting. We are suggesting that this characteristic should not be limited just to effective therapists but that everyone can benefit by practicing empathy.

Even though we feel it is virtually impossible to know precisely what it is like to be inside the shoes of another human being, by practicing empathy, one can certainly move in the direction of understanding—and understanding leads to acceptance.

In interview after interview, we heard people say that by hearing the real stories of others in community building circles, they could begin to empathize with them and then begin to accept the way they were. If more people could just have the patience and compassion to listen openly to other's stories, we could begin to bridge some of the difficult gaps that we chronicled in Chapter Two about the growing isolation and disconnection that people are experiencing.

One of the primary changes reported by participants in workshops was that they experienced an increase in the importance of listening to the stories of others in order to understand them better. What we have learned is that all people have had painful things happen to them, however good they may be at covering it up and the key to building meaningful relationships with others is to be able to share that pain. Carl Rogers said, "That which is most personal is most universal." The secret of participating in groups is that by stripping away the surface stuff and getting to the "most personal" stuff, we find the similarities that bind us together.

Meditation for embodying the principle of Empathy:

Today I will do my best to empathize with others rather than judge them, and honor and accept the ways in which they are different from me.

6. The Principle of Congruence

If you remember nothing else from reading this book, try to hold on to and embody the principle of congruence. In Chapter Five, we defined congruence as essentially alignment between the feeling, experiencing self (authentic self) and the way we act in order to get along in the world (social self).

The literature on acceptance and psychotherapy, both individual and group, is literally teeming with evidence of the therapeutic benefits of living more congruently or authentically. Yet, as we have tried to show in Chapter Four, it is a difficult principle to embody in this culture of conditional love, where social masks and the self-blame/judgment system operate so pervasively.

It takes both courage and discipline to live authentically. It takes courage like that demonstrated by Ray in Chapter Ten, who went from the mainstream of a college campus to being the gardener at a church in a small town so he could follow his call and help people cope with dying. Some of the bravest human beings we have ever encountered are those whose stories fill these pages and others who continue to attend community building workshops and/or support group meetings in church basements and community centers throughout the country.

In a world where most people continue to live "conditional" lives and continue to rely on external reinforcement to feel accepted, living authentically can seem almost like an impossibility. For to do it means one must have the intestinal fortitude that the Buddha displayed in the town square when, in the face of violent opposition, he chose not to accept the "gift" of criticism and scorn (see Chapter Six).

It means being able to sit in a group of people and allow deep, often painful wounds that have been repressed into the unconscious to surface into awareness so that it can be carried by others.

It means being able to identify the various and sundry social masks we wear as a defense against the judgmental and painful attacks of others. And finally, practicing the principle of congruence means being able to discern where and with whom to lower those social masks, revealing the essential, authentic self that lies behind it.

It may be helpful to remember that while God is no respecter of persons, people are respecters of persons and they will judge you for having the unmitigated audacity to actually express how you feel in an authentic manner and ignore how others may feel about it.

Therefore, living authentically is an ongoing challenge in discernment. But in deciding for yourself when and where to be authentic, consider that God not only does not respect worldly status, especially that which is done for the sake of self-aggrandizement, but wants us to follow our authentic call regardless of its effect on worldly status. So does one choose worldly status that will make him or her popular and possibly wealthy among the people who are "respecters of persons?" Or does one choose to follow and act on that which emerges from within, regardless of its worldly applications?

The choice is clear. Choose that which emerges out of love and from deep discernment within and you will be on your way to living a congruent, authentic, fulfilling life.

Meditation for embodying the principle of Congruence:

Today I will pay close attention to what I am feeling on an emotional, physical and spiritual level and I will honor and respect those feelings whatever they may be.

7. The Principle of Purposefulness

This principle is about following your call. One must look inward on a regular basis and ask the question "what am I called to do" or "is what I am doing directly related to my call?" We believe that it is no accident that you or any of us are here. The mistake often made is to follow the call of capitalism or of a charismatic leader or a fad. If you are following a fad, you cannot possibly be following your call because human beings are much more complex and unique than that. We need to heed the advice of Dr. Peck and avoid "doing violence to the subtlety of God's creation" by employing labels to people and by not honoring the differences we see in each other.

What many of us seem to fear is following the uniqueness of our own makeup. As long as we continue to need external reinforcement, we will remain prisoners to the winds of cultural change and the trends that are driven by powerful technology like television that is constantly competing for our attention:

And in the flickering light and the comforting glow
You get the world every night as a TV show
The latest spin on the shit we're in, blow by blow
And the more you watch, the less you know
Beyond the hundred million darkened living rooms

Out where the human ocean roars
Into the failing light the generations go
Heading for the information wars.

—Jackson Browne
("Information Wars," from the album "Looking East")

In order to resist the powerful forces of technology and the information wars, we must detach and look inward more than outward to find our call. The paradox to living purposefully is there is nothing people both respect and revile more than an inner-directed, purposeful human being who knows where he or she is going and doesn't care what others think.

The purposeful human gains respect for having the courage, like the knights in King Arthur's court, to go into the dark forest where there is no path in search of their own way; they are reviled because most of us lack the intestinal fortitude to risk going our own way, plunging into the unknown and so we become envious of those who can and consequently judge them.

Mediation for embodying the principle of Purposefulness:

Today I will affirm my calling and be purposeful in taking steps toward following it. I will also resist following the call of others who may try to persuade me to follow their call.

Conclusion

It may seem odd that a book that begins with a chapter that attacks the culture of rugged individualism ends with a call for more inner-directed, purposeful, independent action. While these two concepts seem at odds with one another, they really are not. Rugged individualism, on the one hand, holds that we should be not only independent and self-contained, but also capable of living alone or with only a handful of others. The Marlboro Man is a false myth. The concept of "rugged individualism" addressed in Chapter One most often leaves a person ragged rather than rugged.

The principles of acceptance, on the other hand: emptiness, openness, unconditionality, inner-directedness, empathy, congruence and purposefulness are important to embody so that one will be able to better connect with others in community. They are means to an end, not an end unto themselves. The end is community.

It is possible for each of us to make choices for health and wholeness when we are alone or even when we are in hostile environments. But what these stories have shown is that community often produces an "explosion" of health and wholeness in individuals. Community can be transformational. One reason for this is that acceptance of one another creates a "space" where healing can occur.

People speak, with wonder in their voice, of how acceptance in the kind of community we have described here has enabled them to walk away from years of harmful behavior toward themselves or toward others. They weren't fixed by others, they were accepted by others. There is a healing power that comes through acceptance.

Barbra Streisand, in a recent interview, was recalling the days when the song "People" was a big hit. She remembered a fan coming up to her during this time and saying "I think you got the lyrics wrong when you sang: "People—people who need people—are the luckiest people in the world." The fan said, "Didn't you mean to say, 'People who don't need people are the luckiest people'?"

There is a widespread feeling that people have been so beaten up by each other that it may not be worth the energy, patience and empathy required to develop meaningful relationships.

More than ever before, people are living alone and having relationships through machines: television, computers, the

Internet, VCRs, e-mail. Many more are choosing pets over people; witness the bumper sticker that says, "The more people I meet, the more I like my dog." This is not exactly a ringing endorsement about the state of human relationships in modern society.

The problem with the trend toward isolation, as we describe at the beginning of this book, is that human beings are incurably social creatures. And no matter how sophisticated our communications technology gets, it will never be a substitute for direct human contact. Technology may be helpful in linking people back up, now that it has so successfully helped to separate us. But it will never replace human relationships.

The hope for humanity lies in rebuilding a sense of community using the techniques and tools found in this book and developed by people like Scott Peck and organizations like the Foundation for Community Encouragement. But we want to be clear: there is no one way to find connection and meaning, just like there is no single best organization or guru or even book.

What works for one person may very well fail for another. It is the recognition of the wildly different nature of human beings that makes development of meaningful relationships so challenging. But becoming aware of the challenge brings us a lot closer to meeting it, and stripping away the differences that lie at the surface of who we are will reveal that which we all have in common.

Our challenge to you is to continue to search for the universal truths that link all of humanity together. We hope this book provides a beginning to that journey. We look forward to meeting you as fellow travelers along the road to acceptance.

Love God, and the person in front of you.

—Reverend Eloy Cruz (Carter, Living Faith*)*

Recommended Reading:

Carter, Jimmy. 1996. *Living Faith.* New York: Times Books - Random House.

Fleming, David L., ed. 1988. *The Christian Ministry of Spiritual Direction.* St. Louis: Review for Religions.

Lewis, C.S. 1943. *Mere Christianity.* New York: Macmillan Publishing Company.

Morneau, Robert F. 1992. *Spiritual Direction: Principles and Practices.* New York: Crossroads.

Nichol, Donald. 1984. *Holiness.* San Francisco: HarperSanFrancisco.

Epilogue

In the Foreword I explained that the mission of the Foundation for Community Encouragement is to teach the principles of healthy communication within and between groups. The authors of this book have described a number of such principles: "Speak when moved"; "Don't speak when not moved"; "Use 'I' or 'my' statements rather than making generalizations"; "'Empty' yourselves so you can listen"; and so on. When people start practicing these principles, as the authors point out, they slowly begin to "tell their stories" authentically and empty themselves of judgment so they can truly hear each other's stories. As this telling and hearing escalates, it naturally evolves that people's acceptance of themselves and of each other also escalates. What the authors have done is to capture this natural evolution of acceptance.

There are some caveats. The principles—or rules—of healthy communication, which FCE teaches, are complex and paradoxical. One of the principles might be stated, "There is an exception to every principle, including this one."

Here are some examples of the way this complexity and paradox have arisen specifically regarding the matter of acceptance:

I used to co-lead an occasional workshop. In the midst of one that was especially thorny, one of the participants said something quite disruptive. A second participant criticized him for it. A third then criticized the critic: "We're supposed to become a community, and in community everything is acceptable." Abandoning my usually neutral stance, I practically exploded: "Everything is not acceptable in here! One of the ways a group becomes a community is by learning what is acceptable community behavior and what is unacceptable. Deliberate deception or violence, for instance, is unacceptable."

As another example, I was the guest of a "call-in" TV talk show and one of the callers asked me about "unconditional love." "I'm not sure there is such a thing," I answered, "except on the part of God for us humans. Many parents may seem to unconditionally love their infant child, but this is predicated on the fact that the infant is theirs. Moreover, as soon as that infant becomes old enough to talk back to them, their love will surely seem conditional. I happen to be involved in leading groups into something we call 'community,'" I went on. "When a group reaches community, it does so only because the group members have accepted each other and themselves in the context of a number of conditions."

My third example is best illustrated by the only other piece of serious research that has been done on FCE's work. In 1991, David Goff, Ph.D., studied graduates of community-building workshops, using as a control group, graduates of a single workshop of similar duration managed by a different organization with a different aim. (This study is abstracted in Goff's chapter "Getting Along Together: The Challenge of Communities" in *Community Building: Renewing Spirit and Learning in Business,* Kazimierz Gozdz, ed. [San Francisco: New Leaders Press, 1995]) One of Goff's findings was of particular interest to me: While the control group reported experiencing a somewhat greater degree of community spirit than the FCE group, the latter reported experiencing a far greater increased awareness of interpersonal differences. In other words, people in the FCE group had managed to reach a state of community more through the *acceptance of their differences* than their celebration of commonality.

This finding is important because we humans *are* different. One's sense of feeling accepted is most often the result of being accepted by others "as we are." It is easy to accept people who are like ourselves. But real acceptance is derived from being appreciated for our real selves, for our uniqueness—accepted precisely because of our differences.

How can people learn real acceptance in just two or three days? How do they learn to discern between appropriate and inappropriate community behavior, and to love and accept each other despite their differences? I have said it is because they are gently taught a system of communication principles. Yet how can such complexity —such delicacy—be taught in a brief period of time? The answer is in one principle that is more fundamental than all the others—the principle of Emptiness.

Essentially the participants are asked to empty themselves of whatever it is that stands between them and community. Most of these are human universals: prejudices; instant liking or disliking of others; inability to listen, particularly to matters that are painful; fear of silence; the self-centered need to fix, heal, or convert; the need to control; and so on. Other things that need to be emptied are exquisitely personal: intense anger at a family member; guilt at having neglected their children; preoccupation with an illness; a habit of sarcasm; a fear of being found out; even a fear of being accepted; and so forth.

It would be impossible for so many to empty themselves of so much in such a short time were it not for FCE's primary value of integrity. The message is: "We will see to it that the group pressure is not such as to cause you to desert your personal integrity." One of the key phrases in our mission statement encourages holding on to the essential and letting go of the unessential. It is amazing how much "baggage" people can empty themselves of as long as they are assured they can—indeed, should—hold on to their integrity. And it is as they let go of such baggage that the cycle of self-acceptance and the acceptance of others spirals ever higher and more widely.

Given that FCE's mission is to teach the principles of healthy group communication, willy-nilly, this means we are teaching a new "culture," a complex system of interlocking rules, or norms, that determines the characteristic behavior of a particular group, be it a family, a business or a nation.

In this book, an example of a group learning a new culture is described in Chapter Nine, on Carlisle Motors. A majority of Carlisle's 600 employees have participated in community-building workshops. Recently, the company developed a "one-price, no negotiating" policy for selling its cars. What an extraordinary "culture shift" for a car dealership in the competitive American marketplace—particularly for an already successful dealership, and even if the change should prove to be only temporary! The very word dealership implies that it should cut "deals." Such a shift evolved out of the company's new culture, and insofar as community-building services contributed to the development of that new culture, it has evolved only because the company had the courage to explore and use those services.

I find this development of a new, highly civil culture heartening, given that we live in a time of cultural breakdown. During this breakdown, doing away with old cultural norms (such as racism and sexism) is often to the world's benefit (though not always, such as doing away with the old norm of balancing national budgets). While I suspect the current cultural breakdown represents a necessary, albeit messy, time of transition, it is also profoundly unsettling and potentially dangerous. Some in academia glory in this transition as a vital phenomenon, a post-modernistic freedom. However, post-modernism espouses that there should be *no* cultural norms: "anything goes"; and this strikes me as nihilism, which has been a diabolic voice through the ages. Many millions the world over simply don't know how to behave any more, whether it be as parents, employees, managers, citizens, or government leaders. The resulting chaos manifests an escalating incivility throughout the world.

The development of a new, highly civil culture, as was done in our small example, is one that virtually all the older cultures could "buy in to." FCE has conducted successful workshops with blacks, whites, Hispanics and Vietnamese; with the wealthy and impoverished; not only in the U.S. and Canada but also in Great Britain, Australia, South Africa, Russia, Taiwan, and Pakistan. When we established our foundation, none of us consciously had such grandiose aim. Yet I see the essence of FCE's work, together with the work of its clients and some other organizations, forging the outlines of a new culture for the planet.

The new culture outlined is not simplistic. It does not declare anybody or everything to be acceptable. Relative to older, traditional cultures, it is complex and paradoxical. But in its complexity and value of paradox, it offers flexibility. I believe it will prove to be a culture of realistic, yet genuine, civility—a culture that encourages respect for one another and a culture that, in the ways the authors have demonstrated, nurtures acceptance.

—M. Scott Peck, M.D.

Appendix A

General Survey of Participants in a Community Building Workshop—Selected Findings

About This Study:

- 200 general participants randomly selected who had attended workshops between 1993 and 1995.
- 31 individuals (15% sample) filled out a 307-question survey between April 1 and May 15.
- 9,500 data points were entered into the database.

Demographics of Respondents:

Educational Attainment	
Post Graduate Work (19)	64%
College Graduate (9)	30%
Trade/Technical (2)	6%

Gender	
Male	43%
Female	57%

Do each of the following phrases describe you: Very Well, Fairly Well, Not Very Well, or Not At All?

On a Spiritual Journey	
Very (26)	84%
Fairly (5)	16%
Not Very (0)	0%
Not At All (0)	0%

Introvert	
Very (14)	45%
Fairly (9)	29%
Not Very (5)	16%
Not At All (3)	1%
Don't Know (0)	0%

EXTROVERT	
Very (5)	17%
Fairly (8)	27%
Not Very (15)	50%
Not At All (2)	1%

RUGGED INDIVIDUAL	
Very (6)	20%
Fairly (15)	50%
Not Very (9)	30%
Not At All (0)	0%

COMFORTABLE REMOVING MASK

(% answering "Very" or "Fairly")

	Before	Now	Change
Best Friend	90%	93%	(3.3%)
God	86%	100%	(16.3%)
Yourself	79%	100%	(26.6%)
Spouse	70%	89%	(27.1%)
Significant Other	67%	66%	(-1.5%)
Co-workers	52%	89%	(71.1%)
Acquaintances	47%	83%	(76.6%)
Parents	41%	93%	(126.8%)
Boss	38%	64%	(68.4%)
Stranger	34%	60%	(76.5%)
Neighbor	26%	66%	(153.8%)
Average	57%	82%	(43.3%)

IMPORTANCE OF:

(% answering "Very" or "Fairly")

	Before	Now	Change
Living Authentically	94%	100%	(6.3%)
Accepting Others for Who They Are	87%	100%	(14.9%)
Accepting Yourself for Who You Are	87%	100%	(14.9%)
What Others Think of You	81%	48%	(-40.7%)

	Before	Now	Change
Listening to the Experiences of Others	71%	100%	(40.8%)

SIGNIFICANT BARRIERS

(% answering "Very" or "Fairly")

	Before	Now	Change
Hard to find people you can trust	65%	32%	(-50.7%)
Fear of Being Judged	61%	13%	(-78.7%)
Fear of Being Rejected	55%	10%	(-81.8%)
Feeling Misunderstood	52%	16%	(-69.2%)
Unable To Lower My Defenses (Social Mask)	48%	0%	(-100.0%)
Too Shy	42%	21%	(-50.0%)
Fear of Appearing Weak	35%	1%	(-99.81%)
No Opportunity To Meet People Interested In Connecting	30%	16%	(-46.6%)
Average	48%	13%	(-72.2%)

CONGRUENCY

(% answering "Very" or "Fairly")

	Before	Now	Change
Strangers	41%	85%	(107.3%)
Acquaintances	50%	90%	(80.0%)
God	80%	100%	(25.0%)
Yourself	90%	100%	(11.1%)
Neighbor	38%	79%	(107.9%)
Best Friend	76%	100%	(31.6%)
Significant Other	62%	100%	(61.9%)
Co-workers	62%	100%	(61.3%)
Boss	52%	79%	(51.9%)
Spouse	63%	100%	(58.7%)
Parents	57%	93%	(63.2%)
Average	61%	93%	(52.9%)

CONNECTEDNESS
(% answering "Very" or "Fairly")

	Before	Now	Change
Stranger	14%	50%	(257.1%)
Acquaintances	45%	66%	(46.6%)
God	84%	100%	(19.0%)
Yourself	87%	100%	(14.9%)
Neighbor	25%	39%	(56.0%)
Best Friend	79%	93%	(17.7%)
Significant Other	67%	89%	(32.8%)
Co-workers	59%	83%	(40.7%)
Boss	43%	65%	(51.1%)
Spouse	58%	100%	(72.4%)
Parents	52%	76%	(39.5%)
Average	55%	78%	(40.6%)

Appendix B

CARLISLE MOTORS SURVEY OF PARTICIPANTS IN A COMMUNITY Building Workshop—Selected Findings

About This Study:

- 325 Carlisle Motors employees were invited to participate in study.
- 135 employees (41.7% sample) filled out a 200-question survey between August 15 and September 15, 1996.
- 27,000 data points were entered into the database.

DEMOGRAPHICS OF RESPONDENTS:

EDUCATIONAL ATTAINMENT	
Post Graduate Work (7)	5%
College Graduate (22)	17%
Some College (29)	22%
Trade/Technical (38)	29%
High School (35)	26%
Less Than High School (7)	5%
Decline (2)	2%

GENDER	
Male	64%
Female	36%

Do each of the following phrases describe you : Very Well, Fairly Well, Not Very Well, or Not At All?

DEEPLY RELIGIOUS	
Very (16)	12%
Fairly (45)	35%
Not Very (42)	33%
Not At All (25)	19%
Don't Know (6)	4%

Private Person	
Very (22)	17%
Fairly (50)	38%
Not Very (44)	33%
Not At All (15)	11%
Don't Know (3)	2%

On a Spiritual Journey	
Very (19)	15%
Fairly (32)	26%
Not Very (31)	25%
Not At All (42)	34%
Don't Know (10)	7%

Introvert	
Very (6)	5%
Fairly (30)	25%
Not Very (44)	37%
Not At All (38)	32%
Don't Know (17)	13%

Extrovert	
Very (27)	23%
Fairly (46)	38%
Not Very (40)	33%
Not At All (7)	6%
Don't Know (15)	11%

Rugged Individual	
Very (14)	11%
Fairly (55)	43%
Not Very (35)	27%
Not At All (24)	19%
Don't Know (7)	5%

How would you rate your feeling of connectedness to the following people before the community-building workshop and now?

FEEL CONNECTED
(Percent answering "Very" or "Fairly")

	Before	Now	Change
Yourself	89%	98%	(10.11%)
Spouse	88%	93%	(5.68%)
Parents	87%	94%	(8.05%)
Significant Other	83%	90%	(12.05%)
Co-Workers	79%	94%	(18.99%)
God	75%	83%	(10.67%)
Boss	63%	81%	(28.57%)
Acquaintances	57%	77%	(35.09%)
Neighbor	52%	72%	(38.46%)
Stranger	21%	48%	(128.00%)
Average	69%	83%	(29.57%)

Rate the following in terms of the barrier it presented to your connecting with others immediately before the community-building workshop and now.

SIGNIFICANT BARRIERS TO CONNECTING
(Percent answering "Very" or "Fairly")

	Before	Now	Change
Feeling misunderstood	37%	11%	(-70.27%)
Fear of being judged	41%	13%	(-68.29%)
Unable to lower my defenses (social mask)	46%	15%	(-67.39%)
Too shy	39%	15%	(-61.54%)
Fear of rejection	36%	14%	(-61.11%)
Fear of weakness	20%	12%	(-40.00%)
Hard to find people to trust	65%	32%	(-50.77%)
Fear of people seeing me as I really am	26%	15%	(- 42.31%)
No opportunity to meet others outside the workplace	41%	29%	(-29.27%)
Average	39%	17%	(- 46.67%)

Rate the following in terms of importance to you immediately before the community-building workshop and now.

THE IMPORTANCE OF:
(Percent answering "Very" or "Fairly")

	Before	Now	Change
What others think of you	73%	58%	(-20.55%)
Accepting yourself for who you are	71%	95%	(33.80%)
Accepting others for who they are	69%	88%	(27.54%)
Living authentically	66%	91%	(37.88%)
Finding meaning in your life	62%	88%	(41.94%)
Learning about the experiences of others	53%	81%	(52.83%
Material possessions	52%	42%	(-23.81%)

How would you have rated yourself in terms of congruency between how you felt (authentic self) and how you acted (social self) immediately before the community-building workshop and now?

CONGRUENCY
(Percent answering "Very" or "Fairly")

	Before	Now	Change
Spouse	72%	78%	(8.33%)
Parents	70%	81%	(15.71%)
Yourself	70%	88%	(25.71%)
Best Friend	68%	81%	(19.12%)
Significant Other	67%	81%	(20.90%)
God	65%	79%	(21.54%)
Co-workers	61%	86%	(40.98%)
Boss	59%	82%	(38.98%)
Neighbor	46%	70%	(52.17%)
Acquaintances	43%	71%	(65.12%)
Strangers	38%	60%	(57.89%)
Average	60%	78%	(33.31%)

How comfortable did you feel removing your social mask immediately prior to the community building workshop and now with the following individuals?

COMFORTABLE REMOVING MASK

(Percent answering "Very" or "Fairly")

	Before	Now	Change
Yourself	81%	99%	(22.20%)
Best Friend	80%	95%	(18.75%)
Parents	80%	97%	(21.25%)
Spouse	77%	92%	(19.48%)
God	77%	91%	(18.18%)
Significant Other	74%	93%	(25.68%)
Co-workers	54%	93%	(72.22%)
Boss	53%	81%	(52.83%)
Neighbor	37%	69%	(86.49%)
Acquaintances	34%	71%	(108.8%)
Stranger	25%	52%	(108.0%)
Average	54%	85%	(50.4%)

Please indicate how well each of the following descriptions reflects the atmosphere of your particular workplace environment immediately before the community-building workshop and now.

WORKPLACE

(Percent answering "Very" or "Fairly")

	Before	Now	Change
I am very loyal to the owners/ managers	94%	96%	(2.13%)
I enjoy the people I work with	91%	95%	(4.40%)
Personal productivity is high	79%	89%	(12.66%)
Workplace has a high degree of teamwork`	65%	86%	(32.31%)
Workplace has a lot of turf battles	61%	43%	(-29.51%)
Easy to communicate openly and honestly with co-workers	57%	88%	(54.39%)
Low motivation	15%	16%	(-6.67%)

About the Authors

Doug Shadel is a consumer advocate and the author of consumer-education materials and programs, which have won 14 national awards. His previous books, also published by Newcastle, are *Schemes and Scams,* and *Outsmart Crime.* Currently, Shadel is the Western regional consumer affairs representative for AARP. He has a doctorate in Educational Leadership. Shadel lives in Seattle, with his son Nicholas.

Bill Thatcher has led a number of nonprofit organizations and has facilitated community-building workshops all over the world. Having served as the executive director of the International Christian Media Commission for the past ten years, as this book goes to press, he has accepted the position of executive director for the Foundation for Community Encouragement. Thatcher has two daughters, Tauryn and Whitney, and lives in Seattle, with his wife, Jane.

We welcome your comments and stories.
You may send correspondence for either
Doug Shadel or Bill Thatcher to:
P.O. Box 17247
Seattle, Washington 98107